PRENTICE-HALL

Foundations of World Regional Geography Series

PHILLIP BACON *and* LORRIN KENNAMER, *Editors*

GEOGRAPHY OF ANGLO-AMERICA, *Loyal Durand, Jr.*

GEOGRAPHY OF NORTH AFRICA AND SOUTHWEST ASIA, *Paul W. English*

GEOGRAPHY OF THE U.S.S.R., *W.A. Douglas Jackson*

GEOGRAPHY OF EUROPE, *Vincent H. Malmström*

AUSTRALIA'S CORNER OF THE WORLD, *Tom L. McKnight*

SOUTHEAST ASIA, *Joseph E. Spencer*

AFRICA, *Donald Vermeer*

GEOGRAPHY OF LATIN AMERICA, *Kempton E. Webb*

Geography
of
Latin America
A REGIONAL ANALYSIS

KEMPTON E. WEBB

Professor of Geography,
Columbia University,
Director,
Institute of Latin American Studies

PRENTICE-HALL, INC., Englewood Cliffs, N.J.

Contents

Illustrations

Foreword

For most dwellers of the Anglo-American realm it comes as a revelation to note that Latin America does not lie to the south at all, but far to the southeast. For many it seems inconceivable, for example, that Antofagasta, on Chile's Pacific coast, is actually east of the meridian that passes through Boston on our own Atlantic seaboard. Further, the airline distance from Buenos Aires to Capetown, South Africa, is less than to Mexico City or New Orleans. But, obviously, it is not simple location or even the great physical and biotic diversity that marks the special association of features that give character to the unique piece of space that we call Latin America. Its personality emerges as the result of both cultural and physical processes that have been in operation through time. While its physical surface is geomorphologically a reflection of the recent as well as the ancient, Latin America, in the context of its cultural surface, similarly exemplifies an almost kaleidoscopic representation of the past and the present in its intricate blending of Indian, Spanish-European, African, and, more recently, North American, components.

Who, in fact, are these folk who are also Americans? In school geography we have so long persisted in labeling the diverse lands and cultures of Latin America as "our friendly neighbors to the south" that we have doubtless infested the popular mind with a bias and a stereotype that has seriously eroded real understanding. Latin America, with its more than two hundred million people and its twenty nations is a far cry from the homogeneous unit that we have tried to make it.

This lack of homogeneity is a function of both time and space. And it is with both time and space that the author concerns himself in this thoughtful and incisive contribution to the Prentice-Hall World Regional Geography Series. Out of this skillful combining of the continua of time and space emerges an evolutionary view of landscape and culture that affords the reader a conceptual framework for viewing this important cultural realm.

Kempton E. Webb is uniquely qualified to prepare a monograph that can provide for its reader an intelligent and original vision of the components that make Latin America a clearly identifiable culture region. His undergraduate degree was earned at Harvard College and his doctorate (1958) at Syracuse University where he studied with the dean of Latin American scholars, Professor Preston E. James. Webb began his academic career at Indiana University and since 1961 has been with Columbia University where he is now Professor of Geography and Director of the Institute of Latin American Studies. He has been Contributing Editor of the *Handbook of Latin American Studies* since 1959 and is the author of many articles on the economic and cultural geography of developing areas—especially Latin America and, more particularly, Brazil. His books include *Geography of Food Supply in Central Minas Gerais* (1959), *Brazil* (1964), *Latin America: A Geographical Commentary* (1966), and *The Changing Face of Northeast Brazil* (1972). In addition to his apparent teaching, writing, and administrative skills, Professor Webb's dedication to field study and his facility with the languages of his region bring to this work those special insights that only come to those who truly know the place and the people—the essence of cultural regional geography.

PHILLIP BACON
University of Houston

LORRIN KENNAMER
The University of Texas, Austin

**Geography
of
Latin America**

CHAPTER 1 *introduction*

What is Latin America? A place, an area, a people? It would be accurate to describe Latin America as a specific area of the earth's surface: the part of the Western Hemisphere that lies south of the continental United States. However, this tells us little about the unique personality of this region.

In more dynamic terms, Latin America is the product of a combination of physical and cultural factors which, interacting over time, have created a unique landscape of distinctly Latin New World character. The reader is asked to consider the man-habitat relationships neither from an environmental-deterministic nor a cultural-deterministic point of view, but rather to focus on the interaction of three elements: land, culture, and time. Landscape characteristics in any given area vary from place to place in different periods for different reasons. The way in which man uses the land modifies the landscape, producing a new environment in which new decisions about land use are made. Frequently these fundamental decisions are based on traditional uses of land, on folk beliefs about certain qualities or attributes of areas and activities, or on a rigid system of sharecropping, to name just a few possibilities. Thus cultural predispositions as well as physical reality influence man's perception of his environment and thereby his activities. This concept of landscape evolution can be stated simply as follows.

The cultural and physical processes that shape any landscape interact continuously, in varying degrees of intensity, with each other, and also with the earth's surface; this surface becomes altered, thereby presenting a continuously changing base upon which subsequent interactions occur.

Let us therefore approach Latin America as one of the major culture

1

regions in the world and try to analyze and interpret it from a geographic point of view.

For a conceptual framework, we may use the analogy of a fabric for the landscape and culture of Latin America, and then identify the various threads which comprise the fabric, the nature of its loom, and the way in which the threads are interwoven to form the fabric.

The Amerindian (American Indian) Thread

This thread refers to the indigenous inhabitants of the New World (Western Hemisphere) before the arrival of Western Europeans around 1500 A.D.; it also refers to their culture or ways of living, and to their skills and tools.

Who were these people and where did they come from? The earliest inhabitants of the Western Hemisphere are believed to have crossed over from Asia by way of the Bering Strait around 40,000 years ago. This was a period when the most pronounced effects of Pleistocene glaciation were diminishing. Although their hunting and gathering culture was simple, these Mongoloid peoples were able to survive in the rather harsh climates of North America. In the period that followed, they migrated southward and eastward across North America, and eventually made their way along the isthmus of Central America into the South American continent. This migration continued over thousands of years until people ultimately settled in the southernmost tip of South America, Tierra del Fuego.

Through the long and difficult periods of adjustment to different environments, these early inhabitants of the Western Hemisphere evolved different working relationships with the earth. In some areas, they were able to build complex cultures, while in others they remained on the fairly low and simple technological level they brought with them from Asia.

Just prior to the Europeans' arrival in the New World in 1500 A.D., there were four principal centers of advanced Indian culture. One was located in northern Guatemala and the Yucatán Peninsula, the home of the Mayan Indians. Another was in the central highland of Mexico where the Aztecs lived at a later time. A third center was in the Andean Highlands of Peru and Bolivia, the heartland of the Inca Empire. A fourth and less important center of Indian culture was located in the Cordillera Oriental of Colombia where the Chibcha peoples lived.

It is natural to expect that those areas which became the homelands, or culture hearths of these more advanced peoples supported a much denser population than other areas. The four just cited coincide precisely with the areas of highest population density. In a mid-twentieth century overview of the entire Western Hemisphere, some anthropologists have said that, prior to 1500 A.D., the entire population of North America, including Central America, amounted to around four million people, three million of whom were located in the former Aztec and Mayan areas of Mexico and Guatemala; the other million were scattered far and wide

NEW MAYA EMPIRE
(A.D. 1200–1450)
1. Mayapán
2. Chichén Itzá
3. Uxmal

OLD MAYA EMPIRE
(A.D. 300–900)
4. Uaxactum
5. Tikal
6. Palenque
7. Quirigua
8. Copán

TRIBES UNDER AZTEC
DOMINATION (A.D. 1200–1520)
9. Tenochtitlán

Sedentary Chibchas
(ca. A.D. 1500)

Greatest extent of Inca
Empire (A.D. 1200–1532)

centers of indigenous cultures

0		500		1000 Miles
0	400	800	1200	1600 Km.

[After Preston E. James, Latin America, *3rd ed. (Odyssey Press, 1959), pp. 15, 16, by permission of the author and of the Bobbs Merrill Co.]*

over the rest of the continent. In South America the total population was believed to be four million: three million were concentrated in the Peruvian-Bolivian Highlands, which comprised the Inca heartland, and the additional million were scattered over the remainder of that continent. More recent population estimates, based upon projections of early colonial baptismal records and even upon analyses of rates of soil erosion due to overcropping, have led some scholars of Latin America to believe the indigenous population densities were in fact much higher. These later geographers believe there may have been as many people then as there are today. The population of Mexico, for example, may have been around 40 million before the conquest by Cortes. While it is not possible to produce a definite figure of population in the pre-Conquest period, it is fairly safe to discuss the patterns of population distribution mentioned above.

In all of the areas of higher culture cited, there was intensive subsistence agriculture. Since there were few domesticated animals, however, most food animals had to be caught or snared in the wild.

The Inca used terracing, fertilizers, and very advanced methods of irrigation. As most of the other high Amerindian cultures, the Inca were settled in one area rather than continually migrating. They had evolved a division of labor (one of the indices of a higher level of cultural development): some people were employed only in the production of food; others were priests, or soldiers, or tax collectors. Any person who lived under Inca rule farmed a plot of land which varied in size with the number of people in his family; part of his harvest went to the chiefs, part to the priests, and the rest was consumed by the great mass of ordinary people. The Inca Empire witnessed the construction of an excellent transportation and communication system which is commonly referred to as the "Inca Highways" but in actuality was simply an elaborate system of footpaths linking all areas of the realm. At the height of its power, just before the entry of Pizarro and his *conquistadores* in the 1530s, the Inca Empire extended as far north as what is now southern Colombia, and as far south as northernmost Chile and Argentina.

The Mayas were the first of the high cultures of Latin America and they fell into two different periods: the Classic Period (300–900 A.D.) and the Mayapan Period, or New Empire (1200–1450 A.D.). The Mayas are noted for having invented a very accurate calendar system, a simple form of picture writing with pictographs or cartoon-like characters, and the zero and a system of counting by 20s, a vigesimal system as against the decimal system which we use. The Mayas erected an impressive number of monumental buildings, although it appears that the great mass of ordinary people lived in less permanent thatched dwellings. Again, population estimates for the Mayan cities have varied widely over the years. Some writers have felt that the cities were mainly religious centers to which people came at certain periods of celebration afterwards dispersing to their homes in the countryside.

The question of the decline and disappearance of the Maya Empire has intrigued scholars for many years. Most observers feel that probably

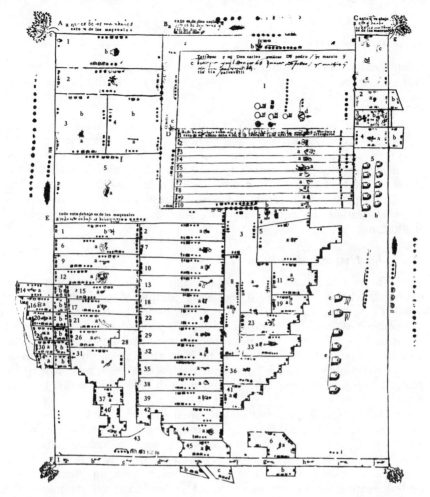

Above: *Detail from the Aztec Oztoticpac Land Map of Texcoco, Mexico (1540), showing property plans. Each field is identified with measurements and glyphs for its Aztec name. The heads at the right indicate the Indian families who farmed these plots.* Below: *An enlarged section showing ten rental plots worked by Indian tenants.* [From Howard F. Cline, "The Oztoticpac Land Maps of Texcoco, 1540," The Quarterly Journal of the Library of Congress, vol. 23 (April 1966), 95, 97.]

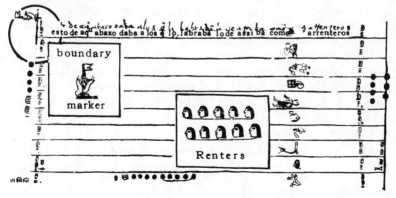

a combination of circumstances such as overcropping, soil erosion, lowered water table, diseases, and warfare, conspired to ensure the Mayan downfall. The descendants of the Mayas are the present-day residents of Guatemala and the Yucatán Peninsula.

One can sum up the characteristics of the Amerindian thread by stressing the cultural diversity and complexity of the indigenous peoples who occupied the Western Hemisphere before the coming of Europeans. There were really many strands to the Amerindian thread, reflecting the different levels of cultural and technological achievements. These earliest Americans provided, in short, a diverse cultural base onto which would later be grafted the equally complex Spanish and Portuguese cultural institutions.

The Hispanic-European Thread

The second thread refers to the Europeans, mainly from Spain and Portugal, who first discovered, explored, conquered, and finally settled what is now Latin America. The reasons for their tumultuous adventuring in the New World will be explained later in more detail. It is important to stress here, however, that these people were seeking riches and fame in a new theater of action which, in their minds, was simply an extension of the Reconquest of their homeland, the Iberian Peninsula, which the Spaniards and Portuguese had wrested from the Moors after 800 years of bloody conflict.

The Spaniards followed closely upon the heels of Columbus' discoveries. Cortes, after realizing the limited possibilities of the West Indies, which was rapidly explored and exploited and its native population decimated by disease, moved quickly onto the densely populated Mexican *meseta*, where the riches of gold and silver held out great promise. A few years later, Pizarro moved quickly into Peru and conquered the Inca Empire.

The Portuguese were slow to follow up their first forays into what is now Brazil. The character of their occupation was different from that of the Spaniards. The Spaniards were interested in precious minerals, converting the Indians to Christianity, and settling on the land granted for participation in the conquest. The Portuguese viewed their New World colony as a rather straight-forward mercantile enterprise whereby the natural resources (unfortunately not including precious minerals at that time) were to be sent to the mother country. Brazil did not have the great appeal and magical attraction which most areas of Hispanic America had.

The essential point is that the Spanish and Portuguese represented an entirely different culture from that of the indigenous peoples they encountered in the New World, and that their European culture would become modified and fused with the Indian cultures they found there.

The Negro Thread

The third thread refers to the African Negroes who were brought to the New World early in the sixteenth century by the Portuguese and

Spaniards as slaves to work the colonial plantations and the mines. These black people came from several different areas of Africa, and like the Amerindians and Europeans reflected a diversity of cultures or sub-cultures. Some of the Africans had knowledge of metallurgy and of crop cultivation which surpassed that of both the Indians and the Europeans. When the Portuguese began sugarcane operations in Northeast Brazil in the early sixteenth century, they depended entirely upon the superior technical knowledge of African Negroes.

The African Negro people added to the Indian and European population of Latin America a new racial element. In some areas like Brazil and the Caribbean, where the highest proportion of black people live, African religious beliefs and practices are very much alive today.

Negro slaves were used not only in the fields, the sugarmills, and in the mines, but also in the households. In Brazil, where the African influence is especially strong, Negro women were servants and nurse-maids. Gilberto Freyre has vividly portrayed this type of family and servant life on the sixteenth century sugar *engenho* in his classic, *The Masters and the Slaves.*[1]

The Negro influence in Latin American music is very pronounced. The distinctive and intricate rhythms of many popular songs and the famous samba and bossa nova are of African derivation.

One of the most important contributions of the African Negro was to expand the diet and cuisine. While the Spanish and Portuguese of the colonial period were content to eat rice, beans, manioc, and beef, the African Negroes tried to balance their diets, whenever possible, with fresh green vegetables and fruits. Many of these foods of African origin were prepared in interesting ways. In some areas, notably in Brazil and the Caribbean, African ways of cooking have been preserved.

The Thread of New World Domesticated Plants and Animals, and Technology

We have just briefly outlined the kinds of peoples and cultural strains that make up the Latin American heritage. Let us now consider the nature of the materials and the technology at the disposal of the Western Hemisphere peoples. We can sum up the stage of technological and material development of the pre-Conquest peoples by stating that they had rich and varied plant materials, but few domesticated animals (compared to Europeans) and a paucity of technological know-how.

The list of domesticated animals is a short one in Latin America before 1500, and most of these were found in the central Andes where at one time or another the llama, alpaca, Muscovy duck, guinea pig, and dog were domesticated. In Mexico turkeys and honeybees were also raised for domestic use. The llama was probably the most versatile of these. It could carry a load of up to ninety pounds, it provided wool and occasionally meat, and its dung was used for fertilizer. The dog was more a scavenger and watchdog than a source of food. Guinea pigs have

[1] New York: Alfred A. Knopf, 1964.

always been (and still are) a feature of Indian cuisine on the altiplano of Peru and Bolivia. The most striking characteristic of all these domesticated animals is that not one among them was capable of pulling a plow, or for that matter, of carrying a man! This meant that if people wanted to go anywhere they had to walk or go by canoe. If they wanted to transport anything, and had no llamas, they had to carry it themselves. It was, in short, a "do-it-yourself" transportation and communication system.

In those areas where crops were planted and not simply gathered (as in the vast tropical regions), the amount of usable land was limited to the area a man could plow and cultivate with a simple digging stick and hoe. Although there were some sophisticated variations on the digging stick in the Andean Inca areas, they did not alter the basically limited character of technology, nor did they extend the possibilities of food production (as draft animals had done in the Old World).

The list of domesticated plants available to the pre-Conquest peoples in Latin America is very long. The number of and diversity of plants, especially beans, compensated in some degree for the lack of meat protein items. Vegetable sauces and condiments enriched and varied the otherwise monotonous diet of the people. New World peoples were the first to domesticate some of the most widely known plants in the world today, such as maize, manioc, and the potato. Maize (or Indian corn) is believed to have been domesticated in the area of the Mexican-Guatemalan border. Its usefulness and versatility is appreciated when one realizes that maize can be used for (1) human consumption and (2) animal feed; can be converted into (3) alcoholic drink; and finally the stalk can be used for (4) fodder. It is an extremely high yielding plant which has been estimated to return about 400 times the amount of seed corn which has been planted. Raising corn is an efficient application of man's labor.

The potato was domesticated in the Peruvian Andes. It started out as a small and rather bitter round tuberous plant (in which form it is still found in that area), but its food value and versatility has been spread around the world. Through hybridization, the potato has become the white Irish potato that is familiar to us today. A list of the more outstanding domesticated plants that were found just in the rich Central Andean area is given in an Appendix.

The tools and techniques at the disposal of New World peoples around 1500 A.D. were simple, unsophisticated, and extremely limiting in terms of building more complex civilizations. We have already mentioned the lack of any efficient plows—due to the simple lack of draft animals to pull them. More outstanding was the lack of the wheel throughout the Western Hemisphere. This meant there could be no mass movement of food supplies into large urban centers—in fact, for this reason, large agglomerations of people in cities were impossible. Nor could there be coach roads or highways, such as the Romans developed in the Old World. The lack of a wheel presented serious obstacles to the transportation of construction materials: neither people nor goods could be moved quickly from place to place. This is all the more curious since what appear to be children's toys with wheels fashioned out of gold and other metals have been found in Peru and Mexico. Apparently the wheel was never applied to the everyday uses with which we associate it because of the lack of draft animals.

Innovations and scientifically advanced principles of agriculture were applied in some of the centers of higher culture, notably in central Peru, where efficient terracing systems were adopted, where water was channeled through stone aqueducts from distant sources, and where fish, animal, and human excrement were used for fertilizer. These were outstanding achievements in agriculture and conservation among the west coast peoples of South America. It is ironic that their descendents in the mid-twentieth century have not been able to continue to apply these principles of soil and water conservation with comparable success. There are very few places in Latin America today where people practice the degree of sophisticated agriculture or exhibit the degree of conservation-mindedness that they did in the area under Inca rule in fifteenth century Peru.

Regarding building construction, there were notable pyramids built in Mexico on the central plateau (e.g., the pyramid of Teotihuacan), and there are also some enormous pyramids in Peru. Buildings which require large interior spaces, however, were impossible because the principle of the vaulted arch was not part of pre-Columbian engineering lore. Only the simple stone lintel was used, as in the Mayan buildings. This kind of "non-arch" did not permit the bridging of large open interior spaces the Romans, and other even older European peoples, had achieved. In short, considering the few devices and techniques at their disposal, one can appreciate how far the Mayan, Aztec, and Inca peoples went with the little they did have. In light of the paucity of their cultural baggage, especially the tools and other *impedimenta* with which a society materially functions, the great number and diversity of useful items the Europeans brought to the New World is all the more impressive.

The Thread of Old World Domesticated Plants and Animals, and Technology

Fifteen hundred A.D. represents the turning point in Latin American history and geography. That date has the magical quality of giving to Latin America the status of a social scientist's paradise. In other words, before the Europeans settled permanently in the New World, there were indigenous cultures with their own tools and techniques. After that date of initial European contact, an entirely new way of life was superimposed on the original peoples. The new settlers brought different languages, tools, laws, plants, animals—in short, a whole new kit of cultural traits. This fundamental turning point or divide in the history of Latin America provides social scientists with one of the few "laboratory conditions" in human history. Tracing the mechanisms and results of that superposition

The Pyramid of Teotihuacan, a massive symbol of the pre-Columbian civiliza-tion, which predates Aztec cultures, in the Valley of Mexico. The volcanic stone structure is 700 feet square and 210 feet high.

of European ways upon the indigenous peoples and their cultures pro-vides an opportunity for some of the most fascinating scholarly sleuthing that has ever been done.

The Europeans brought with them many domesticated plants and animals which proved to be very useful, although some were not adopted by the American Indians to any great extent. The list of plants is striking because it includes many which are familiar to us in the twentieth cen-tury, and it points up the lack of such plants in pre-Conquest Latin America. The Spaniards brought wheat, barley, rice, bananas, and many other fruits and vegetables which we regard as having a worldwide dis-tribution today, but which were nonexistent in the Western Hemisphere before 1500 A.D.

The catalog of animals that the Europeans brought to the New World is equally impressive; it includes all the common barnyard, draft, and stock animals which populate the farms of the entire world today. Horses, chickens, pigs, sheep, goats, cows, and beef cattle were all new to the Latin American scene. This great number and diversity of animals provided the people of Latin America with a potential new source of food, and with the means for pulling a plow. Animal power could now supplement and even supplant human muscle power. A horse and wagon that could transport several people represented a potential of linking the diverse and widely scattered parts of the Spanish and Portuguese realms. Horses and mules really provided the only significant land communication during the colonial period (roughly 1500–1800). Pack trails wound thousands of miles over all parts of the Western Hemisphere, linking those sparsely populated settlements which comprised the toeholds of Western civilization in the New World.

Historians and historical geographers have been interested in why certain European plants and animals were readily adopted by the American Indians and others rejected. It appears that rice, for example, was rapidly accepted because it was a high-yielding plant in terms of the energy and cost expended in its cultivation. On the other hand, grapes were not taken up by the Indians, although the Spaniards were accustomed to drink wine and wanted to grow grapes in such areas as California and middle Chile, whose Mediterranean climate was capable of producing excellent vines. It turned out that the growing of grapes was not an efficient and high-yield activity for the energy expended. Moreover, grapes were not a part of Indian culture and the Indians never acquired a taste for wine. They preferred their own brews, such as *chicha, pulque,* and *tequila,* which were made from native plants.

Wheat grown by the Indians was used mainly as payment in kind for taxes or tribute to the Spanish rulers. The Indians, however, did not take to eating bread made from wheat—they continued to eat corn bread or *tortillas* in Mexico; potatoes, manioc, various squashes, and other indigenous foods elsewhere. On the other hand, beef cattle and sheep were introduced fairly easily. The new livestock did not have to compete with any existing domesticated animals; they could graze on the high pastures of the *altiplano,* on the areas of the *punas* (short grass), and on the *paramos* (long grass) of the Andes; and they provided valuable byproducts such as meat, wool, and hides. The chicken was one newly introduced animal which spread rapidly throughout the Western Hemisphere. In short, the plants and animals that the Europeans introduced provided a much wider diversity of food and fiber materials to the New World inhabitants.

The technology brought to the New World by the Europeans was infinitely superior to that which they found there. They brought the wheel, and a more advanced knowledge of metallurgy. They brought gunpowder and firearms, and construction methods for building large structures with expansive interior spaces. They also brought languages and a system of writing those languages which meant that ideas and information could be stored and transported or communicated across long distances. The closest things to writing which existed among the indigenous pre-Conquest cultures were the pictograph or codice forms of the Mayans and Aztecs and the *quipu* system of knotted strings and ropes by which the Incas kept records and tallies of the stores of grain in their warehouses. These *quipus,* however, could not communicate subtle kinds of information and abstract concepts which Spanish or Portuguese or any other written language could convey.

The superior technology of the Europeans also included shipbuilding and navigation (which accounted for their presence in the New World in the first place!). Their capabilities as ship designers and sailors allowed them to pursue worldwide explorations and, furthermore, to establish permanent overseas colonies. It can be argued that the colonial empires of Portugal and Spain were the most successful in the world. They lasted for over 300 years, an exceptional accomplishment when one considers the limited means and communications facilities available to them between 1500 and 1800.

The Loom of the Physical Environment

It is especially important to clarify the significance of the physical habitat in the development of Latin America. Use of the analogy of a loom for the physical environment suggests that there are certain limitations in the weaving of a fabric: the size of the fabric, for instance, is dictated by the physical dimensions of the loom itself. To carry the analogy further, many different colors and patterns can be woven on a loom by the use and positioning of different threads and by the sequence in which they are placed on the loom.

One of the fixed limits for the physical habitat is altitude. There are few if any permanent human dwellings beyond 18,000 feet above sea level in the Bolivian and Peruvian Andes. The lack of oxygen seems to limit the areas inhabitable by man, and to reduce the growing season to less than 90 days. This limit is emphasized by Bowman in his early writings on the Andes.[2]

There are limits on cultivable areas if man does not have the technology of irrigation available to him. Natural rainfall is simply insufficient to support agriculture in areas such as the Atacama Desert or the *sertão* of Northeast Brazil where irrigation is unavailable. Of course the central and crucial variable here is the culture of the people occupying the area. Preston E. James has stated clearly that the significance of the land in any one place is determined by the altitudes, objectives, and technical abilities of those living there.[3] Other scholars state the idea in other ways. They write that the skills and preferences of the local inhabitants are the determining factors which influence the actual use (and sometimes misuse) of the land.

We view the physical habitat, then, as presenting relatively fixed limits upon human habitation, assuming simple technology, but note that within these limits exists a broad range of possibilities for land occupance which depends upon the culture of the local people. At the same time, the physical characteristics of the earth's surface have changed with time. There has been an evolution of the landscape itself, due to the interaction of physical and cultural processes through time. The concept of landscape evolution states that the cultural and physical processes which shape any landscape are continuously interacting with each other, and also with the

[2] Isaiah Bowman, *The Andes of Southern Peru* (American Geographical Society, 1916).

[3] *Latin America* (Odyssey Press, 1969), p. 37.

earth's surface. When the earth's surface becomes altered, this produces a continuously changing base upon which subsequent interactions occur.[4]

In other words, the very landscape itself is in a state of flux, as are the processes which have shaped that landscape. There are many physical processes of soil formation, of vegetation growth, of climatic change, in addition to the processes of human growth, population settlement, migration, and land use. These processes all interact, to a greater or lesser degree, to produce a landscape which changes in different ways at different times for different reasons.

The widely contrasting aspects of Latin America's surface configuration, climate, soils, vegetation, river systems, and hydrography will be discussed in more detail later. At this point, however, it can be stressed that despite the popular environmental-deterministic outlook, which attributes underdevelopment to the mountainous slopes, poor soils or enervating climate, the evidence buttressed by field observation and historical–geographical research appears to warrant a much more cultural-deterministic outlook.

How else would a civilization such as the Inca Empire flourish in what, to many observers, might appear to be an extremely hostile environment in the Andes: mountainous terrain with slopes of up to 40 degrees, elevations between 11,000 and 15,000 feet above sea level with few flat cultivable areas? How else could one account for the high culture of the Mayas which prospered in the hot humid climate of the Yucatan Peninsula? Or the Aztecs, who fashioned a civilization in a setting deficient in rainfall over most of the year? The physical environment is extremely important in the geographic of Latin America, but we must also consider the cultures of the people who occupy any given area.

The Threads Interwoven:
Miscegenation and Acculturation

The fabric is ready to be woven. The juxtaposition of the various threads of different peoples, different ways of life, and different technologies through time is called the process of acculturation. Miscegenation refers to the intermarriage of people of different races to produce children who have physical characteristics of both parents and, therefore, of both races.

In the early period of the Conquest, the unions of Spanish *conquistadores* with Indian women produced mestizo children. Mestizo children also resulted from the mixing of Portuguese men with the Indian women of Brazil. With the coming of African slaves early in the sixteenth century, the white European men and the Negro women produced mulatto children. Miscegenation also occurred in varying degrees among all three racial elements: Indian, white Caucasian, and African Negro.

[4] Kempton E. Webb, "Landscape Evolution: A Tool for Analyzing Population–Resource Relationships: Northeast Brazil as a Test Area," in Zelinsky, Koscinsky, and Prothero (eds.), *Geography and a Crowding World* (Oxford University Press, 1970), pp. 218–34.

The *cafuso* of Brazil resulted from the union of the African with the Indian.

Today we find populations with predominantly Indian characteristics in precisely the same areas where the Indians were most heavily concentrated in the immediate pre-Conquest period. In the West Indies today, however, there are few people with predominantly Indian racial characteristics: within a few decades of Spanish occupation of that area, there was widespread decimation of the native population due to diseases against which the Indians had little immunity.

Where there were few Indians, or where Indian influence was weak due to decimation by disease or war, as in Costa Rica or Uruguay or Argentina, the Caucasian or white European became the dominant racial type. In coastal Northeast Brazil where sugarcane cultivation prompted the bringing in of many African slaves, there is today the highest incidence of mulattoes and other part-Negro people of greater or lesser degree of Negroid characteristics within Brazil. Similarly, along the shores of the Caribbean sea, there are many mulatto peoples. The largely mestizo and mainly Indian populations are found in southernmost Mexico and Guatemala (the former Aztec and Mayan areas), and also in Ecuador, Peru, and Bolivia (the former Inca homeland).

Acculturation is the blending of different cultures. It is a two-way process by which the European culture of the Spanish and Portuguese conquerors became the dominant one but in which there was also a reverse movement in the direction of Indian cultural elements. Indigenous foods such as manioc, maize, and potato were quickly adopted by the Europeans and eventually used throughout the world. Often an Indian language was used as a *lingua franca* in the early colonial period before Spanish or Portuguese could be imposed more completely; and some are still spoken today by people in these areas, although many Indians speak at least some Spanish.

It is helpful to remember that the principal ingrediĕnts of the cultural mix in Latin America were combined in uneven proportions. In some areas, because of the Indians' almost total rejection of European ways, it is probably more accurate to refer to the juxtaposition rather than imposition of European with indigenous culture. Miscegenation and acculturation characterize the ongoing processes of adaptation and mutual adjustment that have been operating in Latin America ever since the Conquest, and whose later phases are operating even today.

The Historical-Geographical Process of Landscape Evolution

In any culture realm such as Latin America it is necessary to relate past with present and future. The historical approach tries to bring the facts and events of the past to bear upon those of the present and, hopefully, upon the outlook for the future. In Latin America, we deal with the continuum of time, in which we share with the historian a curiosity about cause and effect, and the sequence of events through time. We are also concerned, and possibly even more concerned, as geographers, with the spacial continuum where the focus is upon the significance of differences from place to place within the complex culture realm of Latin America. If we combine the two continua of time and space, we can view the specific segment of the earth's Latin American crust as one vast landscape (with its myriad of physical and cultural features) which is evolving through time in response to multiple physical and cultural processes acting upon it. This evolutionary view of the landscape and culture of Latin America affords us a conceptual framework or a way of looking at this important culture realm.

CHAPTER 2 origins and antecedents
of new world settlement

The Extent of the Known World to Western Eyes

It is practically impossible to understand the political, economic, strategic, or even psychological motivations which underlay the discovery and settlement of Latin America without understanding something of the Old World just before 1500 A.D. I am suggesting here that the whole adventure of New World conquest was but an extension of the drama which had been enacted on the Iberian peninsula for centuries preceding 1492 when Columbus first sighted the New World. In fact the discovery and settlement of the New World was the logical culmination of events which began in the early Middle Ages.

In twelfth century Europe the extent of the known world was extremely limited. On the crude world maps of that day it was plain that Europeans knew little of what existed beyond the limits of Europe. Their most accurate notions of place geography centered upon Western Europe and all the lands bordering the Mediterranean Sea. Those vastnesses extending southward into the bleak Sahara wilderness and eastward to the Near East and Far East were beyond the comprehension of Europeans. Theirs was a small closed world, but still large enough to enclose the thought and aspirations of a people whose levels of technical skill and means of communication were severely limited.

Between 1271 and 1295, an extraordinary journey was made by two Italians, Marco Polo and his brother, who traveled to China and back by a land and sea route. Many people believe they were the first Europeans to go to the Far East, although it is more probable that other people had preceded them. The significant thing about their trip is that they published a narrative account of what they saw. The *Travels of Marco Polo* excited wide interest in Europe regarding the East. Europe had long

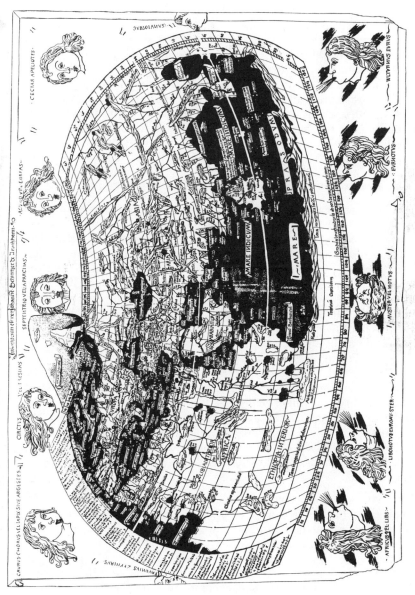

A Map of the World according to Ptolemy (From the Latin edition of Ptolemy's geography published at Ulm in 1482, after the original in the New York Public Library, Lenox Branch.)

received a trickle of costly spices, scents, silks, and other low-bulk-high-value commodities which found their way (through the Moslem merchant middlemen) by caravan across the arid wastes of the Near East and by sailing ship across the Mediterranean Sea to Venice and Genoa. The importance of the spices and perfumes is sometimes underestimated in our twentieth-century world, but the fact remains that spices were more than a condiment in the Middle Ages. They were a means for covering up the taste or smell of putrefying food; the perfumes were substitute baths, which had not yet become a daily, weekly, or even monthly event in the regimen of most Europeans. These spices and perfumes were such valuable commodities that Europeans began to consider the possible ways of establishing direct trading ties with the East, thereby avoiding the Moslem middlemen.

The Renaissance and Man's Expanded Horizons

The awakening of Western Europeans to new lands to the East was further stimulated by the general renaissance (literally rebirth) which much of Europe enjoyed in the fifteenth and sixteenth centuries. The Renaissance represented an expanding of man's horizons, and more importantly, a change in man's concept of his place in the universe and the world around him. Prior to the Renaissance, Western man had seen himself as a passive element in a vast universe in which he had no power or will to control his own destiny.

The Renaissance was, moreover, a period of innovation in tools and techniques of ship design and navigation which enabled Europeans, especially the Portuguese and later the Spaniards, to venture beyond the familiar haunts of the Mediterranean Sea and the coastlines of peninsular Europe. This newfound freedom afforded Western Europeans a sense of partial mastery over their environment and imbued them with ambition and purpose to shape their own lives and, indeed, to shape the affairs of other men. It is within this context of self-confidence, purpose, and will that the voyages of discovery were possible. Europe was ready, by virtue of its tools, skills, and attitudes, to discover new and different worlds, and indeed did.

THE VOYAGES OF DISCOVERY (1420–1620). During most of the fifteenth century, the Europeans' knowledge of the world continually expanded as a result of the courageous and sustained explorations by the Portuguese and Spanish discoverers.

Prince Henry the Navigator of Portugal (1394–1460) is the first person to have pursued geographical exploration on a systematic and long-term basis. As a boy he had accompanied his father on military campaigns against the Moors and had gone as far south as Cevta, which lies on the northernmost tip of northwest Africa, just across the Straits of Gibraltar from Spain. Henry's thirst for adventure and his consuming curiosity about unknown areas led him to contract with ship owners to have the African coastline explored. All through the middle decades of the fifteenth century Portuguese ships slowly pushed southward along Africa's west coast until about half of it had been visited and charted by the time of Prince Henry's death in 1460.

The Portuguese were the champion sailor-navigators of that era. By 1430 they had discovered and claimed the Azore Islands in the North Atlantic and had moved on to Northwest Africa. Prince Henry contracted with a number of ship owner-captains to explore 100 or more leagues of African coastline within a fixed time period, a system designed to minimize the element of risk. Even so, there were many difficulties. The counter winds and currents of the South Atlantic made southerly probing difficult. On several occasions the ship captains were more interested in finding ivory, gold, and African slaves, than in exploring.

This systematic geographical exploration was continued after Prince Henry's death and, in 1497, Bartholomeu Dias reached the Cape of Good Hope. Although he returned directly to Portugal, one of his successors, Vasco da Gama, rounded the Cape and reached Calicut in 1498. The Portuguese established forts and trading posts along the coast of East Africa and India, and realized their hopes of commercial domination in the Far East and East Indies for at least the following one hundred years.

Christopher Columbus, the Italian navigator who sailed for Spain, also hoped to reach India, but by sailing in the opposite direction, the west. His theory was correct, but instead of arriving in the Far East he discovered a whole new hemisphere. Pedro Alvares Cabral, a Portuguese, landed in Brazil in 1500 on his way to India, and in 1519, Magalhães (Magellan), another Portuguese, circumnavigated the world, although he did not live to complete the journey.

It could be said that most of the fifteenth-century explorations involved the rounding of Africa and the reaching of the Far East by the Portuguese. That brief period between 1490 and 1550 saw the circumnavigation of the world and also the coastwise probing of most of the Western Hemisphere, including Latin America as well as most of Anglo-America. In other words, by 1550, the outlines of the Western Hemisphere were pretty well known. The remaining seventy years of the Age of Discovery (1420–1620) were devoted to filling in the blank areas on the Western Hemisphere map. There has never been a period comparable to the Renaissance Age of Discovery, during which man's knowledge of the world expanded at such a rapid rate!

THE RECONQUEST OF THE IBERIAN PENINSULA FROM MOORISH OCCU-PATION. We have seen how the physical expansion of Spain and Portugal into Latin America was made possible by a combination of technological developments in shipping and navigation, and by changes in the attitude of Western Europeans. A more specific motive for the Iberian settlement of the New World stemmed from the Reconquest of their own peninsula from the Moslems.

The early Iberians were a mixture of Celts, Swabian Central Europeans in the northwestern corner of the peninsula, people from the Roman occupation (vandals and others), and Visigoths subsequent to

Roman occupation. These diverse strains of cultural stock contrasted sharply with the alien culture of the Moors who invaded the Iberian peninsula in 711 and remained for almost 800 years until they were expelled from Granada in 1492.

The long occupation by the Moors left a permanent influence on the Iberian peninsula. At the time of the invasion, Moorish culture was superior to that of the Europeans in many ways. The Moors had institutions of higher learning and great libraries; a highly developed technology, including techniques of water management and irrigation; and an advanced system of civil and property laws.

The Moorish influence was most pronounced in southern Spain, weakest in northwestern Spain and northern Portugal. Parts of Galicia, in fact, were never completely dominated by the Moors, just as they had never been by the Romans.

The Spaniards fought a continual battle against the Moors. The Christians believed their central mission was to expel the infidels, or nonbelievers, from their land. The Portuguese, who were mostly small independent farmers, were less involved in fighting. Since the business of conquering was a matter of securing towns and roads, the Moorish domination had little effect on people who lived outside the towns and away from principal roads.

The men who took arms against the Moors were motivated by a combination of economic and religious sentiments. Many were without land, capital, or family influence, and they were paid for their services as "soldiers of the true faith" with grants of land. Thus soldiering was an important avenue of upward social and economic mobility. These hopes of economic reward helped to buttress their religious fervor in expelling the Moorish infidels and, later, motivated the *conquistadores*.

It is a striking coincidence that the expulsion of the Moors coincided exactly with the Spanish discovery of the New World. To the *caballeros* who were, so to speak, unemployed as of 1492, it was welcome news that Columbus had found a New World with infidels, or Indians, who could be converted to Christianity. Their experience in conquest and settlement guided the Iberian conquerors in their exploration and consolidation of the New World territories.

CHAPTER 3 *the process of new world settlement*

The Strategy of Settlement

Historians and other students of Latin America spell Conquest with a capital "C," a proper noun justified by the rapid and brilliant manner in which an unbelievably small number of Europeans managed to subdue an enormous unknown area occupied by literally millions of people. How was this incredible feat accomplished? By what rights did the Spaniards lay claim to large areas of the Western Hemisphere?

In 1492 and 1494 the Treaty of Tordesillas was signed through the offices of the Pope: the two competitors, Spain and Portugal, agreed to concentrate their explorations in certain areas of the world, and particularly in the Western Hemisphere. A north-south line was drawn 370 leagues west of the Cape Verde Islands passing close to the mouth of the Amazon. By the terms of the treaty, lands east of the line were to be explored and colonized by Portugal; lands west of it, by Spain. It was a "Catholic gentleman's agreement" made without any consideration of what other countries might want. Although the Treaty of Tordesillas reinforced their drives to territorial conquest, the Spaniards strongly believed that they merited legal ownership to South America because of their arduous exploration and occupation of it. Furthermore, the Spaniards believed that they had the rights to those areas of the New World where they had "Christianized" the native Indians. These were merely the extension of attitudes fostered during the Reconquest of the Iberian Peninsula, as previously mentioned.

The legal concept of *uti posidetis* proved to be a forceful influence in the conduct of Spanish affairs in the New World: in other words, possession constituted ownership, and the mere occupation of an area gave substance to any claim of ownership. It was, in fact, this notion of *uti*

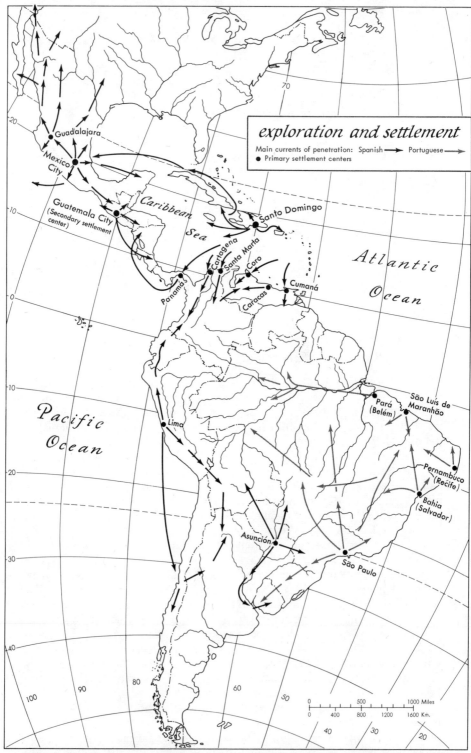

The Exploration and Settlement of Latin America   [After Preston E. James,
Latin America, 3rd ed. (Odyssey Press, 1959), pp. 18, 20, by permission of the
author and of the Bobbs Merrill Co.]

posidetis which eventually allowed Brazil to claim the vast Amazon basin west of the Tordesillas Treaty line because that area was occupied by Portuguese-speaking people. This was the crucial argument which eventually gave those lands to Brazil, although the boundaries were not finally negotiated until the nineteenth century by the Barão de Rio Branco in one of the outstanding diplomatic negotiations of frontier delimitation in the Western Hemisphere.

The Conquest was accomplished by small groups of Europeans, accompanied by many Indians, who made long marches or short forays out into the unknown. One particular group consisted of 30 Spaniards, an army of 3000 Indian bearers, and around 350 swine. The bearers carried the food supplies, arms, and personal accoutrements; the swine were slaughtered for food. The Spanish captain and his lieutenants usually wore armor as a symbol of rank. The guns they carried were noisy and impressive, and the other steel weapons, pikes and spears, were far superior to any Indian weapons. The Spaniards also had their war dogs— large, ferocious, hungry-looking animals—that frightened the Indian adversaries. In the early years of the Conquest there were few horses and actually mules proved to be better than horses for the rugged work.

In addition to technological superiority, the Spaniards had a tremendous psychological advantage over Indians who had never before seen a European, much less an armored Spanish soldier on horseback. At first, the Indians believed the man and horse were one complete animal. When the man dismounted, the animal appeared to have come apart. Imagine their dismay at this spectacle, and their fright at the blast of the Spanish blunderbusses! These crude guns scared the Indians more than they killed them.

The Europeans were single-minded; they fought with conviction and confidence in the face of overwhelming numerical odds. The Indians, on the other hand, evinced too little initiative and individualism and they gave up easily. The Spaniards soon learned to kill or capture the chief in any battle, whereupon the rest of the Indian soldiers lost heart and fled. Some writers have explained the consistent Spanish victories by pointing to the fact that the major battles occurred during the harvest season when most Indians were more interested in gathering their maize crops than in doing battle with the foreigners.

Hernando Cortes organized his expedition in 1519 from Cuba. From there, he landed in Mexico and established a base at Veracruz. He even burned his ships to prevent any possibility of his troops turning back. Upon reaching the central plateau of Mexico, Cortes and his small band of two hundred men were amazed to see the wealth and pomp and monumental buildings of the Aztecs. The Aztec emperor, Montezuma, tried to bribe the Spaniards with gold, but this only whetted their appetites for more booty.

Cortes and his men fought numerous battles against the Aztecs and their allies. In the bloodiest, and most critical battle, fought for control of the Aztec capital Mexico City, the Spaniards suffered heavy losses. When they finally won, the Spaniards rebuilt Mexico City, Spanish style, directly on the foundations of the destroyed Aztec temples and other important buildings. This was a symbolic political and religious reconstruction in which the old order was replaced by the new Spanish order of the *conquistadores*. From then on, the frontier of Spanish occupation advanced over a long period. From Mexico City, the Spanish lines of conquest and occupation moved northward toward California and southward into Central America.

Cortes had many political and administrative problems in making a cohesive whole out of the enormous area of Mexico (New Spain, as it was called). He was also intent upon acquiring an even larger territory under his own jurisdiction. In attempting this, he was being insubordinate to Velasquez, the governor of Cuba who commissioned the expedition in the first place. Velasquez contested Cortes' deeds by appealing to the Crown, but the gold which had been sent to Spain apparently convinced the king to support Cortes' jurisdiction over Mexico. Later on, the king sent a special viceroy to Mexico to establish an *audiencia,* an administrative body representing the Spanish Crown. From the decisions of this body and others in Spain, the *conquistadores* were allowed their personal wealth but they were obliged to give up their governing rights to the areas they had conquered.

The history of the Conquest of Mexico illustrates that the Spaniards' attitudes toward the New World had become strongly focused upon the three things they greatly desired: gold, land, and Indians who could be enslaved to work in the mines and fields.

When Balboa crossed the Isthmus of Panama and discovered the Pacific Ocean in 1513, he was accompanied by Francisco Pizarro, who had served several years in the Caribbean area. Pizarro carried forward Balboa's exploration and worked his way southward. With a small band he finally reached Peru in 1531, and saw evidence of the high culture which the Inca had established. Pizarro returned to Spain to get the authority for conquest in order to assure that his rights and privileges would be honored. He then returned, and with about 180 men and 27 horses, captured the Inca king Atahualpa. Through a fortuitous coincidence of internal strife and a power struggle within the Inca governing family, Pizarro was able to take over. The Spaniards melted down into bullion most of the gold booty they took.

Despite a number of Indian revolts in subsequent years, Spain had succeeded in dominating the two great high culture areas of the Western Hemisphere, Mexico, and Peru. From these two principle governing centers, other secondary centers of settlement were located in Guatemala, Colombia, Chile, and Paraguay.

The strategy of Portuguese settlement was quite different in that the Portuguese neglected in large part their New World claim. The Portuguese did not find much excitement in what is now Brazil. They did not find gold; the Indians were hunters and gatherers who had not built an impressive civilization. Moreover, the Portuguese were involved in a very profitable trade with the Far East. What they did manage to establish, however, were the *feitorias,* or trading posts, which were simple forest clearings that were gathering points for the dyewoods (the *pau brasil* from which the name for the country came). The *feitorias* were located along the coast of Northeast Brazil and in the Amazon area. Sugarcane cultivation became a more stable and profitable activity in the 1530s and actually provided the single outstanding form of wealth in Brazil until around 1700. The Portuguese were not as zealous in trying to convert the Indians; moreover the Indians were not adaptable to Portuguese aims. There was, in short, little similarity between the Spanish and Portuguese strategies of settlement.

In their patterns of settlement, the Portuguese clung to the coast at a few toeholds, since they needed access to navigable water in order to ship out the bulky brazilwood and sugar. Any interior expeditions went directly inland from the coast and there was no attempt to build overland communication linking the coastal settlements. Travel was by water for the most part. It was not until later in the sixteenth century with the decline of Portuguese influence in the Far East that the mother country cast a more interested eye upon her New World territories.

The Portuguese faced special financial and military problems in securing their claim to Brazil. For example, it took large amounts of money from Portugal to operate the *feitorias* and to get the brazilwood out. Furthermore, the Portuguese were harassed by the French who, not subscribing to the Tordesillas division of the world, had the unfriendly habit of capturing Portuguese ships.

The Instruments of Latin American Occupation and Colonization

The means by which the Portuguese seized and consolidated their Brazilian territory was the donatory system. The coast of Northeast Brazil was divided into fifteen strips of land (captaincies) extending inland from the coast. These lands were given to twelve donatories, essentially feudal lords, who were granted many privileges; in return, they had to invest their own money in the land. Only five of the original fifteen donatories were successful; success or failure depended upon the Indian population there, the resources of the area, and the skills with which they were exploited. By 1549 the Portuguese Crown decided to take back some of the power it had given the donatories. A central governorship was set up and the donatories lost their governing powers but they retained their economic power and wealth. The system of the donatories was only partially successful.

By 1548, Brazil had only sixteen different settlements, compared with the much greater number of settlements in Spanish America, which had been developed as early as 1538. The Portuguese settlers were harassed by the French who tried to settle in what became Rio de Janeiro in 1555; in 1560 they were driven out, and Rio was established as a Portuguese military garrison in 1567. By 1570 there were only about thirty thousand civilized people in Brazil, including certain groups of Indians regarded as civilized by the Portuguese. In general, the Portuguese occupation consisted of small independent settlements which were not welded together into an effective cohesive unit until much later.

The underlying philosophy of Spain and Portugal toward their New World colonies was based on mercantilism, which can be defined as the benefiting of the mother country at the expense of the colonies. The American colonies were to supply the raw materials that would be shipped to the homeland for processing; and they were expected to buy the goods manufactured from these materials. Mercantilism required a strong merchant marine and navy to effect and protect the trading. In the years following the Conquest, however, there was, understandably, such great interest in getting gold bullion to Spain and Portugal that ordinary commerce suffered.

The similarities between the Portuguese and Spanish colonial systems were:

1. Both had a highly centralized authority in the Crown of the mother country, with pronounced regulatory control in both colonies.
2. Both societies had a rigid class system, which everyone accepted. People of the lower classes were awed by the apparatus and accoutrements of the upper classes, and these feelings tended to reinforce their sense of inferiority.
3. Both mother countries were Roman Catholic.
4. Both pursued a policy of mercantilism including all types of monopoly.

The significant differences were:

1. Spain was much more powerful than Portugal.
2. Portuguese interests were mainly concentrated in Asia.
3. The Portuguese colonies included no Indian nations such as the Aztecs and Incas, with highly-developed cultural institutions, nor was any gold found in Brazil in the early colonial period.
4. The Church was much stronger in Spanish America than in Brazil.
5. The Spanish had a more complex system of administration.

There were many theories and plans of government for the New World colonies, but the actual day-to-day administration followed these rules only in a token sense. Many of the regulations sent out from Spain were impractical. Appeals to the authorities in the mother country took too long: often the local colonial official would have to take action long before the reply arrived. It is important to remember that the Spanish crown—the sovereign ruler in person—was the overlord of Spanish America.

The instruments of occupation were diverse. Mines, missions, forts, and plantations were the centers of colonial development in the New World. The mines, in the strategy of Latin America, were a continuation of former Indian operations. The missions were set up primarily to aid the military and exploratory expeditions in extending the zone of European influence. Forts, the remotest European outposts, were bastions against possible attacks by hostile Indians or European rivals. Finally, the plantations, such as those where sugarcane was cultivated in Brazil, not only generated revenues for the mother countries, but also acted as an effective means of occupying areas that did not have the attractions of valuable mineral resources.

At this point it may be useful to point out some of the problems in Spain's colonial administration. (*1*) All members of the colonial administration except town councilmen were appointed in Spain. (*2*) Most of the income from America was used in administering the American colonies. (*3*) Terms of office were limited to an average of three years. (*4*) Executive, legislative, and judicial functions were all exercised by one body, the *audiencia*. This overlapping of authority made it difficult for the average person to get satisfaction in his encounters with Spanish colonial officialdom. Some individuals would cut through the red tape by using influence and bribes. The ultimate authority in all matters resided in the Spanish Crown. That is where appeals went, and where the ultimate decision of the *residencias* came from. Anybody who wanted to could communicate directly with the Crown; in this way the Crown encouraged spying from officials who reported on each other to Spain.

There were certain policies to prevent Spaniards from becoming "Americanized." Officials were shifted around, in the manner of the present day U.S. Foreign Service transfers, so that they would not get too attached to a particular place or special interest groups. There were pressures against marriage and association of Spaniards with Creoles (persons of Spanish descent born in the New World). Spaniards were prohibited from buying property in the New World.

Everything was done to make the peninsular Spaniards superior to the Spanish Americans. Creoles were frequently asserted to be inferior to Spaniards, an inferiority blamed upon climate, diet, and Indian blood.

A strong alliance developed between ecclesiastical and civil administrations. The Crown used the Church to spiritually weld the colonies to Spain and also to perform many administrative functions (the census data of that era were essentially the baptismal records of the churches). The Church censored reading materials, discouraged gambling, and strongly attempted to control thought. In general, a complex and comprehensive administration was set up in the New World.

Just how did the Spanish Crown profit from the New World adventure? Its profits were mostly revenues from the following:

1. Excise taxes on internal colonial trade, export and import taxes, especially on *pulque* (a native alcoholic drink), official paper, salt, matches, and other necessities.
2. A sales tax, the *alcabala*, of two to six percent (from which the Church was largely exempt).
3. A customs duty tax, an ad valorem tax amounting to fifteen percent of the value of the item.
4. A head tax paid by the Indians as a form of tribute; those who lived in *encomiendas* paid it to their Spanish *encomendero*. [An *encomendero* was a man who by royal favor was given the right to use a given area of land (*encomienda*) which included the right to the labor or tribute of the inhabitants there.] It was a nominal amount.

5. The *quinto* or "Royal Fifth," a twenty percent tax on precious metals, mostly gold. After the gold dust brought in to the royal foundries was melted down, a fifth of it was removed, with the remainder stamped to signify that the tax had been paid.
6. Control of freight movements by peninsular Spaniards, and not Spanish Americans, so that money earned from trade enriched Spain rather than the colonies.
7. Salaries of colonial military and civil posts paid by the New World territories, not by Spain—an additional way that the Crown saved money.

These taxes were not really very onerous. The real burdens were the limitations of mercantilism on economic activities, and the tradition of "aristocratic dispensation." The latter accounted for a great inequality of treatment, low per capita income, the difficulties of transportation, the low amounts of capital available, and the unwillingness of Spain to invest in the New World. Another institution which evolved as a response to the heavy controls of Spain against commerce was smuggling. Contraband, possibly the oldest economic activity in Latin America, was a response to the harsh trade restrictions. Tax exemptions were used as incentives for new business ventures, especially in poor or high-risk areas. The *alcabala* (sales tax), for example, was less in America than in Spain.

Tax incentives are an old institution that has survived to the present day. In the 1960s, for instance, Brazil has reduced taxes as much as fifty percent for firms that invest in such capital-hungry areas as the Amazon and Northeast Brazil. Possibly a more important point to remember, however, is that there was no land tax whatsoever in Latin America, essentially another example of aristocratic dispensation. To some extent this tradition has persisted to modern times, for even today, where land taxes are assessed, they are ridiculously low. (I observed in Northeast Brazil in 1964 a cotton and cattle *fazenda* of fifty square miles that paid fifty dollars per year in taxes. And even at that, the *fazendeiro* complained about rising taxes!)

In sum, the occupation of Latin America was a complexly engineered and administered system, dominated by economic motives and buttressed by a vast government machine involving the Church, the military, and social institutions. This is why the colonial experience was such a success for over three centuries.

Changing Definitions of Resources in Latin America

It is apparent when we look back over the early formative years of Latin America's occupation and colonization that there was a unique cultural definition given to resources of that area and time; in other words, Spain and Portugal considered that the resources in sixteenth century America consisted mainly of gold and a few raw materials. Over subsequent centuries it is possible to trace a slow change in the definition of resources in Latin America.

Even in the mind of the average North American a paradox exists. Most schoolchildren are taught that Latin America (which they often confuse with South America) is a land of "vast untapped resources." At a slightly later age they learn that Latin American countries are poor, and that many Latin Americans live in abject poverty, only exceeded by that in certain Asian countries. Hence the paradox: If Latin America is so rich, why are the Latin American people so poor? Without attempting to explain the gaps in the North American educational system regarding the study of Latin America, some observations regarding the essentially cultural nature of resources are appropriate here.

We have already pointed out the ways of analyzing landscapes, and of observing how landscapes have changed through time. We can further view landscapes as a reflection of resource definition by particular cultures. In other words, an informed "reading" of a landscape tells us much about the culture of the people who occupy it, how they regard the land, how they use and misuse it. Throughout the European occupation, the processes of landscape evolution in Latin America have accelerated in random rather than constructive, conservationist ways. At the same time, the local Latin American conceptions of resources have remained relatively static. These traditional conceptions of resources hold (1) that the ownership of land per se is a good thing, hence the *latifundio* and low land tax rates; (2) that work can best be accomplished by large numbers of low-paid workers; and (3) that financial gain is greatest in a closed market situation with little competition and with windfall profits from speculating on scarce commodities. In short, gain the most profit in the shortest time, and invest as little as possible of the profits into maintaining the source of income. In other words, reap the harvest without planting the seeds.

The twentieth century presents us with a new situation since there are not only more people now, but these people have access to more and better means of change. Contemporary man is capable of transforming his landscape-habitat at a much faster rate.

Processes of landscape evolution in Latin America have accelerated randomly in nonconstructive ways since European occupation, and local interpretation and perceptions of resources have remained relatively static. The results are distinctly unfavorable: (1) undervalorization of land, and of all physical, technological, and human resources; (2) gross imbalances of living levels and widespread poverty throughout Latin America.

In some areas of southern Brazil, Venezuela, Argentina, and in areas of commercial agriculture in Mexico and Colombia, modern definitions of resources are applied to land utilization. In these areas the efficient allocation of all elements of crop production, including use of fertilizer, soil conditioners, and machinery to maximize the output from that land, represent a mid-twentieth century definition of rational resource use. An important part of this definition is conservation to assure the future productivity of the land.

The key words in the management of resources are productivity and valorization. The ultimate aim is maximum valorization not only of the land, through the use of modern technology, but also of the skills of the people who work the land, so that their productivity can be raised. It is assumed that they will share in the increased yields and incomes, although this is not always true.

The interaction of man and land through time in Latin America implies a continued redefinition of the concept of resources for any given area. And it is the particular association of definitions which is manifested in the distinctiveness of different areas in Latin America.

CHAPTER **4** *the physical setting*

The Shape of the Land

If we look at the Western Hemisphere on a globe, we see some fundamental similarities and differences between North and South America. Central America is the small land bridge between the Isthmus of Tehuantepec in southernmost Mexico and Colombia. Both North America and South America have a roughly triangular shape, apex pointing southward, and broad east-west dimensions in their northernmost latitudes. Both continents have geologically young mountain systems trending north to south in their western portions. The Rockies, the Cascade Range, and the Sierra Nevada punctuate the west of all North America. In South America the mighty Andes form an unbroken zone of high land and steep slopes all the way from eastern Venezuela to Tierra del Fuego. Both continents have geologically older and therefore less rugged mountains. The Appalachian Mountains of the eastern United States have their counterpart in the highlands of Guiana and Brazil. Most broad areas of these eastern highlands in both continents seldom exceed 5000 feet in elevation. Isolated peaks range up to almost 10,000 feet. The highest peaks in the western areas of South and North America rise between 14,000 and 20,000 feet. Mt. Aconcagua (elevation 22,835 feet) is the highest South American peak; Mt. McKinley (elevation 20,300 feet) is the highest North American peak. A third similarity between North and South America is the broad interior lowland formed by the Mississippi-Missouri river systems into which the sediments and detritus eroded from the Appalachians and Rockies are carried and deposited. In South America the broad Amazon and Paraguay-Paraná river system opens an interior corridor which drains the higher lands on either side.

These similarities end abruptly if we talk about climate because of

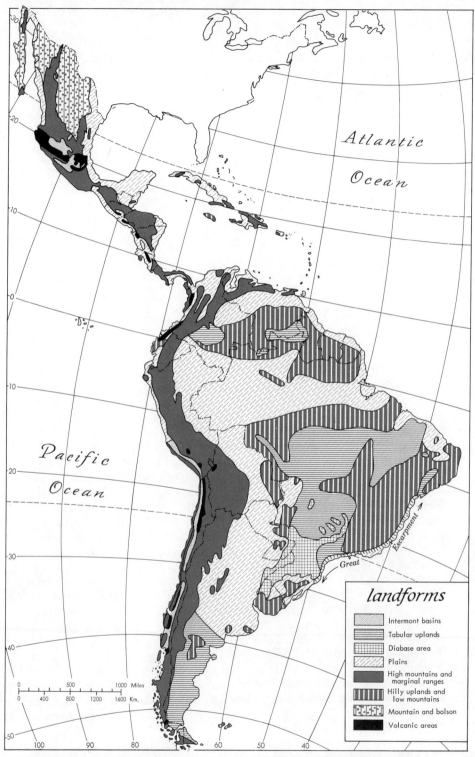

landforms

- Intermont basins
- Tabular uplands
- Diabase area
- Plains
- High mountains and marginal ranges
- Hilly uplands and low mountains
- Mountain and bolson
- Volcanic areas

Atlantic

Ocean

Pacific

Ocean

Great

Escarpment →

0   500   1000 Miles

0 400 800 1200 1600 Km.

Landforms [After Preston E. James, *Latin America*, 3rd ed. (Odyssey Press, 1959), pp. 25, 26, by permission of the author and the Bobbs Merrill Co.]

the latitudes at which the broad and the narrow portions of each continent lie. The narrowest parts of North America are in tropical latitudes whereas the broadest parts are in subarctic latitudes. Conversely, the broadest part of South America straddles the equator and the narrowest portion is found in the higher middle latitudes. This geographical dissimilarity means that the higher latitude areas of North America experience marked continentality of climate with wide temperature ranges between winter and summer, whereas the high latitude areas of South America (latitude 50° south), in Tierra del Fuego, experience maritime climates with as little as 20° Fahrenheit difference between the coldest and warmest average monthly temperatures. The shape and arrangement of the land surface of Latin America is another primary factor in determining the climatic and vegetation groupings.

Although most people are taught that latitude location determines the climate of a particular place, it is the elevation above sea level, exposure, and slope which often prove to be the critical climatic factors, especially in Latin America. The Andes form the single most impressive and obvious physical feature, although it is not a single mountain chain: it is a continuous mass of interconnecting mountain systems exhibiting different characteristics from one area to another. There are the permanent snow- and ice-covered uninhabited zones along the Chile-Argentina border; the broad densely-settled altiplano areas of central Peru and Bolivia; and there are densely populated intermountain basins in the northern Andes of Colombia and Venezuela. The Andes, therefore, constitute not one geographical unit, but many, whose diverse aspects are shaped by the distribution of climatic and geomorphic agents in each area.

The fact that so many Latin Americans live in moderately to highly elevated areas tends to disprove the "conventional wisdom" often expounded upon the effects of climate in the tropics. The vertical arrangement of ecological zones due to the decrease of temperature with increasing elevation means that a wide variety of crops can be grown, thus offering local inhabitants a "smorgasbord effect" of land use options. The accompanying section of Colombia shows the *tierra caliente,* which supports the growing of bananas, sugarcane, rice, and tropical fruits. Between 3,000 and 6,000 feet are the coffee lands of the *tierra templada,* above which lie the cold lands or the *tierra fria* of wheat and barley, and finally above 10,000 feet, the alpine grasslands. In the drier areas of Peru and Bolivia inadequate rainfall precludes the tall *páramo* grasslands of wetter Venezuela and Colombia and Ecuador, and we find the shorter *ichu* grass and *tola* shrub of the *puna.* Permanent snow exists in altitudes of more than 15,000 feet above sea level. This decrease in air temperature, which averages approximately 3.3° Fahrenheit per 1000 feet, is the average lapse rate, or decrease of environmental temperature with elevation. It is caused by the increasing distance from the vast rediating surface of earth which is responsible for heating the atmosphere.

Some observers claim that the Andes pose a barrier to communications. To a limited extent they are correct, for no great arteries of commerce have been attracted to cross that mountainous zone. On the other

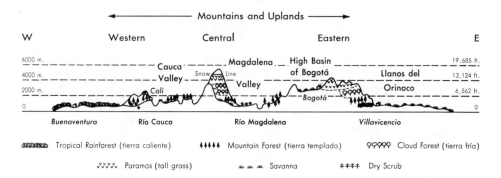

Vertical Zonation of Colombia [*Adapted from Irmgard Pohl, Josef Zepp, and Kempton E. Webb,* Latin America, A Geographical Commentary *(London: John Murray, 1966), p. 173.*]

hand, the Andes do not pose an impassable obstacle. Roads, railroads, and airlines do cross the Andes serving various areas throughout the entire mountainous realm. It is only fair to state, however, that building a railroad or highway through mountains is much more expensive than in flat areas, but mountains are not insuperable obstacles where there is an economic, strategic, or social justification for building a road. The Panama Canal illustrates this point. The strategic and economic advantages supporting the digging of the Canal far outweighed the costs of building it and of maintaining a disease-free zone there. Unfortunately, most humid tropical areas in the world do not provide the social or economic justifications for the vast investments required to create other "Panama Canal Zones."

The land of Mexico is a direct continuation of land forms in the southeastern United States. In fact, the first real discontinuity in geological structures occurs just south of Mexico in an east-west zone of volcanic land forms; another geological boundary forms the Isthmus of Tehuantepec. Interestingly enough, the folded and faulted structures of Central America are closely related to those of the West Indies. Some of the mountains of Cuba and Hispaniola are continuations of east-west structures which have disappeared under the Caribbean Sea only to emerge in the Greater Antilles. Similarly, the easternmost islands of the Lesser Antilles are geologically related to the Venezuelan Andes. Time and space does not permit a detailed exposition of the tremendous diversity of land forms in Latin America. It is safe to say, however, that there is as much diversity to be found there as in any part of the world.

Climatic Patterns

The full range of climatic types is found in Latin America, from the humid tropical climates to the *inlandeis* areas of southern Chile-Argentina Andes.

The principal determinants of Latin America's climate are latitude (thereby determining the angles of incidence of the sun's rays), the arrangement of land and water areas, and atmospheric pressure and patterns which produce wind systems, precipitation, and exposure. We have already seen how the significant difference of South America compared to North America consists of its broad east-west dimensions in the lowest latitudes and the relatively small proportion of land located in middle and upper latitudes.

Although many people believe that Latin America has an unbearably hot climate, the fact remains that the highest temperature of around 110° F is found not in the Amazon Basin but rather in the dry Chaco area of northwestern Argentina and Paraguay and in the similarly dry area of the lower Colorado River close to the U.S.–Mexico boundary. Very low relative humidity—less than 10 percent—also characterizes these areas. In terms of sensible temperature, the Amazon Basin seems to have temperatures higher than its actual range of 70–90°, due to the contributory factor of high relative humidity.

The west coast climates of Latin America are influenced by cold equatorward-flowing currents; the cold California Current in the north and the cold Peru Current in the south. The California Current is the easternmost portion of the North Pacific clockwise whirl of winds and currents and the Peru Current is the easternmost portion of the South Pacific counterclockwise wind and pressure system. These currents, which return the chilled waters from high to low latitudes, maintain a heat balance between lower and higher latitudes. Due to their lower temperature these cold currents stabilize the air above them and prevent it from rising, thereby producing very dry conditions. Coastal Peru and the Atacama Desert of northern Chile are among the driest places on the earth. On those infrequent occasions (every twenty-five years or so) when the Peru Current moves farther out to sea, a tongue of warm equatorial water moves southward between the Peru Current and the shore, disrupting marine ecology, causing torrential downpours, and wreaking general havoc in the area. *El Niño* (literally the Christ Child) is the name given to this spectacular phenomenon because it usually occurs around Christmas time.

The eastern shores of South America are bathed by warm currents; the South Atlantic counterclockwise whirl causes warm water to flow southward along Brazil's coast; and the movement of water northwestward along the northeast coast of South America, in and around the Caribbean Sea and Gulf of Mexico, raise the temperature of the seas in that area. Such warm water seas readily give up moisture to the atmosphere, providing those areas with high relative humidities.

The accompanying Köppen climatic classification map shows the distribution of the larger categories of climates. Although a relatively small proportion of that total area can be classified as humid tropical, the greater proportion by far of even the tropical latitudes has been characterized by wet and dry savanna-type climate. Even within the Amazon, most of the yearly rainfall occurs during the summer rainy sea-

climates

Af, Am =	wet climate, no cool or dry season
Aw =	wet climate, distinct dry season
Bw =	dry climate
Bs =	semiarid
Cs =	wet climate, mild rainy winters, cool dry summers
Cw =	wet climate, mild dry winters, hot rainy summers
Cf =	wet climate, mild winters, no dry season
E =	cool or cold climate, no warm season

Gulf of Mexico

Atlantic Ocean

Pacific Ocean

By the Köppen system, quantitatively defined characteristics are identified by letter symbols; combinations of letter symbols are used to identify climatic types. Here are shown the climatic types found in Latin America, explained by the key above.

0	500	1000 Miles		
0	400	800	1200	1600 Km.

Climates [Adapted from Preston E. James, Latin America, 4th ed. (Odyssey Press, 1969), p. 31, by permission.]

son of six months, while the other six months are relatively dry. In the Aw climate, the so-called rainy season is only two to four months. Some people misinterpret the expression "rainy season" in the context of Aw savanna climates. They think it rains all day long every day during that period. Nothing could be further from the truth. What it means simply is that more rain falls during those months than during the rest of the year. The rainy season may occur, as in Belo Horizonte, Brazil, from November to March, during which there are dry intervals of one or two or three weeks; when the rain does come, it only lasts for a few hours. There is ample sunshine between the showery periods. Even the weather in the humid tropical Af areas of heavy rainfull (up to 80 inches per year) is nothing compared with the bleak succession of 164 interminable rainy days Great Britain experiences even though London's annual rainfall amounts to an average of only 25 inches!

The B or dry climates are limited mainly to western Argentina, the arid coast of northern Chile and Peru, and northern Mexico; there is also a small but impressive B climate area in the interior of Northeast Brazil. The Mediterranean climates, with their winter rains and summer drought, are limited to a small area of middle Chile. The absence of D climates is due merely to the absence of land area in those latitudes (between 50° and 60°) where they would otherwise occur.

Modern air mass analysis and advances in synoptic meteorology have revised our ideas regarding the climatic processes and patterns in Latin America. Not too many years ago, much of the climatology focused upon a belt or linear system, stressing the latitudinal zones of climate. In more recent years, with the gathering of more and better meteorological data from surface stations as well as the upper atmosphere, and especially with the advent of high speed airplanes and weather observation satellites, a more accurate picture of the movements of air masses has revealed that the low latitude areas are influenced by the weather fronts of the middle and higher latitudes. For example, Arctic air masses originating in northern Canada sweep southward across the Great Plains of the United States to bring intense winter cold to the east coast of Mexico in the vicinity of Veracruz. These are the so-called northers. Similarly, the Antarctic air masses which push northeastward past Tierra del Fuego and inch northward along the Argentine coast, eventually move inland along the interior corridor of least resistance, the axis of the Paraná-Paraguay river system, and bring the *friagems* (cold spells) which extend into the upper Amazon Basin. These *friagems* lower the temperature by as much as 15° to 20° F and bring intense discomfort to the local inhabitants unprepared for such a radical departure from the expected temperature.

The range in amount of rainfall is quite impressive. Quibdo, Colombia, has the dubious distinction of being the rainiest place in Latin America with a total average annual rainfall of 415 inches. There are places in the Atacama of Chile, such as Iquique and Calama, where no rainfall has been recorded over a period of several decades. Most of the gradients from one climate to another are gradual where there are no

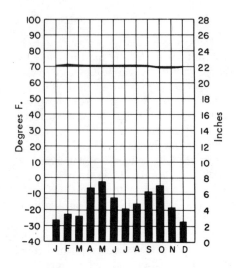

Climagraphs
[*From Howard J. Critchfield,*
General Climatology, *2nd ed.*
(Prentice-Hall, Inc., 1966).]

Medellín, Colombia (4,951 ft.)(1,509 m.)
Average annual temperature   71°
Annual temperature range   3°
Average annual precipitation   58.8"

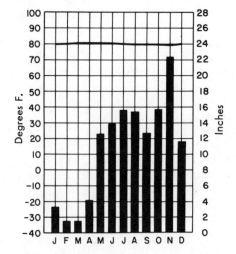

Colón, Panamá (coast level)
Average annual temperature   81°
Annual temperature range   2°
Average annual precipitation   130.3"

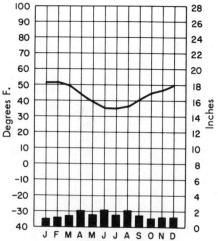

Punta Arenas, Chile (92 ft.)(28 m.)
Average annual temperature   44°
Annual temperature range   16°
Average annual precipitation   19.4"

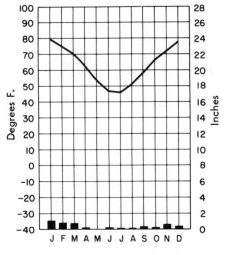

San Juan, Argentina (2,178 ft.)(664 m.)
Average annual temperature   63°
Annual temperature range   33°
Average annual precipitation   4.6"

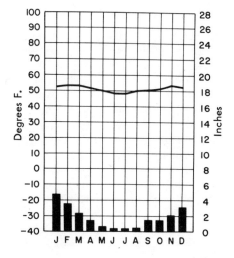

La Paz, Bolivia (12,001 ft.)(3,658 m.)
Average annual temperature   52°
Annual temperature range   6°
Average annual precipitation   22.1"

sharp differences in slope transitions. But, naturally, the rain shadow effect of the Andes between Chile and Argentina is pronounced where the westerly winds drop most of their moisture on the western, or windward, Andean slopes, thus providing Argentina's Patagonia with a semiarid leeward side. There are some striking climatic gradients such as in Northeast Brazil where, proceeding inland from Recife or João Pessoa, one moves from a tropical humid ecology (Af or Am) to a BW desert climate within the short distance of one hundred miles. The accompanying climagraphs and water balance diagrams present some of the climatic variations within Latin America.

An example of the tertiary order (local type climatic phenomenon) is the hurricanes which are spawned over the warm Caribbean waters under extremely unstable atmospheric conditions, and find their way over parts of Mexico and the southern and eastern United States. The diversity of climate provides a broad base for raising many different combinations of crops and livestock. It is a permissive rather than a limiting factor on the ways in which man can use the land of Latin America.

Vegetation and Soils

The single best indicator of overall land quality within Latin America is probably a map of vegetation. This is because the distribution of plants and plant communities reflects the composite conditions of climate, soils, and soil moisture. Vegetation is a useful indicator because it is easily observable and can be photographed aerially or from the ground, thus providing an immediate picture of the ecology of any given area. It is common knowledge among ordinary farmers in Latin America that the quality of the land is indicated by the kinds of trees and plants in the area.

The basic categories of vegetation types for Latin America are shown in the Appendix. There are many ways to classify vegetation. One is to distinguish the barren areas from those covered by plants. The barren areas would necessarily include the driest deserts of northern Mexico and the middle west coast of South America. Within those remaining areas with plant cover, the most basic distinction is between forests and grasslands. Contrary to popular lore, the heavily forested areas of the humid tropics comprise only a fraction of the total land area of Latin America. Equally spacious are the vast subtropical savanna lands or *campos cerrados* of Brazil and the *llanos* of Colombia and Venezuela.

Within the general category of forested areas, there is naturally a greater area covered by low latitude forests of all types including the tropical rainforest (*selva*) as well as the tropical semideciduous evergreen forests and the scrub and thorn forests characteristic of the Chaco, interior Northeast Brazil, and southwestern Mexico. The middle latitude forests are limited to a small area of Mediterranean scrub forest in middle Chile, the more highly elevated coniferous forests of Mexico and central America, and the Araucaria forest of southern Brazil—mainly in the states of Paraná and Santa Catarina. There is a considerably large area of broadleaf and mixed broadleaf-coniferous forest in southern Chile and Tierra del Fuego.

The grasslands are an enigma to persons unfamiliar with Latin America and tropical zones generally because they include the very fertile prairie pampas soils of Argentina as well as the geologically ancient, sterile, acid soils of the *campos* of Brazil.

While the map can provide us with the outlines of major vegetation types, we should try to provide a qualitative guide to the meaning of these different vegetation types. The cultural significance of different vegetation types varies. The common North American experience, for instance, was that of the westward-moving pioneer of nineteenth century United States who equated grasslands with soil fertility once he had the steel plow, barbed wire, the windmill, and the Colt six-shooter to help him valorize it. On the other hand, *mata* or forest in Brazil, is synonymous with rich farmland, and *campo*, or grasslands, with poor sterile soils. When a peasant farmer in Northeast Brazil was asked whether there was any good cropland in the vicinity, he replied, "Yes, we have good forests here." In another area, the reply to the same question was, "No, there is only thorn and scrub forest here." In other words, land quality is evidenced by the types of local vegetation. In most tropical areas the reason for this is the close relationship between soil and plant growth.

It is only under the evergreen semideciduous tropical forest that a humus layer exists. Semideciduous trees drop their leaves one by one throughout the year; the forest litter decomposes and forms a thin layer of organically rich soil. When cleared, this land provides satisfactory yields of shallow-rooted crops for a limited period. If no fertilizers or soil conditioners are used, however, the area will soon lose its fertility and the crop yields will fall to an uneconomical level.

In the tropical heartland of the Amazon, heavy rainfall and high temperatures hasten the chemical dissolution of parent material and many soil nutrients are leached away out of reach to shallow-rooted crops. The extremely tall dense trees there survive only by virtue of tap roots descending to the lower depths, as deep as one hundred meters, where more unweathered materials lie, while the shallower roots draw sustenance from the upper soil horizons. The tropical rainforest thus lives largely upon itself and upon the products of its own decomposition.

As a first order generalization it can be said that vegetation patterns of Latin America approximately parallel the climatic patterns. We find, therefore, the hygrophyllous plants (the lianas and epiphytes) in those areas of Af and Am climate, and the xerophytic or drought-resistant plants in abundance in the drier areas of BW and BS climates. The second and third orders of generalizations apply to local variations according to the types of parent material or country rock. Some of the richer soils within tropical Latin America are found upon the weathered diabase lavas, as in the highlands of Central America and in the *terra roxa* (red earth) coffee areas of São Paulo and Paraná of Brazil. Some limestones, under certain conditions of weathering, produce locally superior agricultural soils. The alluvial deposits of river valleys and delta provide another instance where tropical soils are more fertile than might be expected. The floodplain of the Amazon River, although comprising a mere two percent of the Amazon Basin area, provides virtually the only permanently cultivable land because the annual flooding enriches the soils by additional layers of silt.

What man *does* to the vegetation is another problem. Much of Latin America's history can be written in terms of the quest for forested lands that could be cleared and planted, and subsequently used for cattle grazing. Before industrialization and urbanization, the limited tools available to the average farmer were also limited in their destructive effects on the land. However, with more effective plows, axes, and tractors, man has been able to increase his effectiveness in changing the landscape. The growth of cities has generated a large demand for charcoal, for example. The main source of charcoal is the scrub forest of the interior. Within a few years, whole areas have been cut over, resulting in severe soil erosion on the steep slopes. Conservation techniques by reforestation have been applied in only a few areas and these efforts cannot begin to make up for the widespread destruction which has occurred over most of Latin America's landscape.

In our subsequent examination of the different areas of Latin America we shall try to place a time perspective upon what has happened to the vegetation cover. Eyewitness accounts and diaries of Cortes' footsoldiers tell of the dense, almost luxuriant forests in the Valley of Mexico. In every instance, there was a denser cover of vegetation in the earlier colonial period than now. One can compare photographs taken fifty and even twenty years ago, and find an observable and marked decrease in the density of the vegetation cover.

The alteration of soils in Latin America goes hand in hand with that of the vegetation. Unfortunately, the mapping of soil types is not as easy as vegetation mapping; in only a few areas has any soil mapping been done. One aspect of soils which is significant to agriculture is the basis upon which soils are distinguished as arable or nonarable. In industrialized areas of the world where farming is mechanized (high capital inputs, low labor inputs) and produces high yields per man hour expended, arable land is defined as that which can be farmed with a tractor; that is, land with a slope of less than 8 degrees. Arable land in Latin America, on the other hand, includes any area where a man with a hoe can stand, sometimes precariously, and cultivate a field or small garden patch. There are many instances in Mexico, Central America, and the Andes, where slopes of 20, 30, and even 40 degrees are farmed. What happens, of course, is this: when land is cleared and burned over at the end of the dry season, when it lies bare and exposed to the elements, the first rains wash away the topmost layer including its valuable nutritive organic compounds. Further aggravating this harmful exposure of open fields on steep slopes is the fact that most farmers in Latin America plant their maize, beans, and manioc in rows running up and down the slope, and not along the contour. These rows hasten the water runoff and it does not take long for small rivulets to become gullies. It is a sad spectacle to witness the soil resources of a country washing away. The ecological balance, in short, is being radically altered. With faster clearing of slopes and erosion of soil, the runoff rate is increased. This means, furthermore, that the fluctuations of stream levels between high and low become wider.

I witnessed the flooding of the Rio Pelotas, which forms the boundary between Rio Grande do Sul and Santa Catarina in southern Brazil, after particularly heavy snows and rains in July and August 1965. The level of the river rose by 40 meters (over 130 feet). This is possible only with a large volume of water and a deeply entrenched, narrow river valley. It is but one isolated manifestation of man's influence over his habitat and his lack of control of the entire process. That flooding river, which tore out a new reinforced concrete bridge, was the bitter harvest of almost 400 years of wanton destruction of vegetation cover and the erosion of soil through wasteful cropping and grazing practices. The outlook is not encouraging.

River Systems

Nature played a cruel trick on Latin America when the rivers were laid out. It is ironic that such a large segment of the earth's surface which is amply provided with rainfall for the most part, is so poorly endowed with usable, navigable waterways. Some casual observers have tried to see a parallel between the Mississippi River and the Amazon River. The

Above: *Ten-foot gullies on the distant slope, which has been cleared for maize and upland rice, in southern Ceará.* Below: *Washout of a new bridge over the Rio Pelotas in Brazil, August 1965, due to heavy snows and rains. Deforestation over the past century has increased run-off to the extent that this river rose 130 feet above its low stage. Note the deeply entrenched valley.*

only similarity is that they both carry a great deal of water. Whereas the Mississippi drains a highly productive, rich agricultural heartland and, moreover, serves as a transportation network linking areas and population grouping of extremely high productivity, the Amazon drains a sparsely-populated area, poor in resources and low in productivity. Despite the length and volume of flow in the major branches of the Amazon, many of the southern tributaries are not accessible to large ships because of the rapids in their lower courses just before they join the main Amazon streams.

The Paraná-Paraguay river system has a shifting main channel which can accommodate only shallow-draft ships. Brazil's so-called river of national unity, the Rio São Francisco, has a middle navigable stretch of about 1000 miles, lying between the 300-mile unnavigable stretch including the Paulo Alfonso Falls in the north, and the rapids at Pirapora. The lower 150 miles from Pirapora to the sea is also navigable by small ships. There are no navigable streams at all serving the most populous and productive area of eastern and southern Brazil.

The steep slopes of the Andes are drained by rushing, jumping streams and only some of them in Ecuador, Colombia, and Venezuela have navigable portions between the piedmont of the Andes and the sea. Much of north central Mexico consists of basins of interior drainage and there is essentially no water there, navigable or otherwise. Central America has an East-West asymmetrical topographical section with a short steep slope facing the Pacific Ocean, and a gradual slope descending to the Caribbean. Most of the rainfall occurs on the eastward facing slopes, and the lower portions of those Caribbean-emptying streams are navigable only to very small craft, like canoes.

One might characterize the pattern and operation of river drainage systems in Latin America by saying that they are inconveniently located with regard to the needs of the population. This theme of mismatching of location with need is a recurrent one and we shall encounter it again as we discuss the geography of particular areas in more detail.

The Amazon River is, of course, the river of largest volume and rate of discharge in the world. It defies description because it is more than can be comprehended by a single view of it, even from an airplane. Here are some interesting aspects to it:

1. It is not, as many people would believe, a meandering stream, but rather a river of fairly straight trajectory interrupted by countless lens-shaped islands.
2. The courses of the main channel and secondary channels (*paranas*) do not change as frequently as many people might think. Carbon-dating of black earths on Careiro Island near Manaus by Hilgard Sternberg illustrated the permanence of shoreline occupance sites for 1300 to 2000 years.
3. It is in the Amazon Basin that one observes the black water and white water streams with their respective qualities of low-sediment–high-acid and high-sediment–low-acid characteristics.

The basic research that will enable us to understand this magnificent river has begun only recently.

CHAPTER 5 *population*

Distribution and Density

Certain basic facts impress the observer of Latin America's population characteristics. (*1*) It has the fastest rate of population growth of any continental area in the world. Recent census data indicate that the average rate of population increase is around three percent per year, which is not only higher than that in North America but also significantly above the rate in African and Asia, the other large developing areas of the world. (*2*) The population, as has been noted by Preston James, is distributed in isolated clusters separated by vast, sparsely populated areas.[1] (*3*) Although the rate of increase is extremely high, the total population is relatively low (about 270 million in 1970). The recent surge in population during the twentieth century is mainly attributable to high birth rates during a time when medical technology has drastically reduced mortality rates. Prior to this century, widespread disease took a great toll of lives. Immigration continues, but on a greatly reduced scale: During the nineteenth century millions of Europeans migrated to Latin America (mainly Argentina and Southern Brazil).

As one views Middle America (that portion of the Western Hemisphere between the United States and Colombia), the main concentrations of people are in the highland basins of Mexico, the irrigated valleys of the dry northwest, and in the more fertile basins and valleys of the Central American mountain systems. These densely settled areas are generally those which had the greatest numbers of pre-Columbian people at the time of the Conquest. The Spaniards were attracted to them by their more evolved culture, as represented by the art works of gold and silver which they found there. They were also attracted by the potential labor

[1] Preston E. James, *Latin America,* 4th ed. (Odyssey Press, 1969), p. 4.

force which could be enslaved to work in the mines and on the plantations. The emptiest places in Latin America today are the very driest areas of northern Mexico and the warm humid Caribbean coastlands, excluding the narrow fringe of coastal plantations. The "Mediterranean" area of Middle America, the West Indies, is generally densely settled, while the larger islands of Haiti, Puerto Rico, and Jamaica have some of the highest rural population densities in Latin America.

A population dot map of South America gives the impression that most people live close to the sea. A more careful examination of a larger-scale population map reveals that most people live within one to two hundred miles of the coast—not a shoreline distribution pattern at all. The entire Andean area, with the exception of the southernmost part of the continent, boasts high densities within the protected intermontane basins and valleys far removed from the coast. Principal lines of communications within the Andes run parallel in a north-south direction, except for the coastal trunk road of Peru. Hence the distribution of population clusters assumes a linear form running north-south.

The densest populations of the Andes, then, are found at higher elevations, between 6,000 and 14,000 feet above sea level where the Quechua-speaking descendents of the Incas still live. On the eastern side of South America, most of the people are concentrated within fifty to a hundred miles of the large conurbations of Buenos Aires, Porto Alegre, São Paulo, Rio de Janeiro, Belo Horizonte, Salvador, Recife, and Fortaleza. These cities comprise the national or regional primate cities within which an extraordinary concentration of urban functions occur. For example, the state of São Paulo boasts half of the industrial productive capacity of all Brazil, and the overwhelming majority of that state's industries are in or around São Paulo city. These cities also tend to concentrate social, political, and educational functions and, in turn, constitute great loci of consumer demand. The producers and consumers are limited in large part to these "super-cities." The denser rural populations are found in the interior of Northeast and southern Brazil and the Humid Pampas of Argentina and Uruguay. Vast unpopulated areas exist in the interior of the continent; most of the Amazon Basin and Patagonia are empty of people. It is possible to travel long distances in Latin America and encounter very few people.

Migration

The people of Latin America have always been ready to follow opportunity wherever it went. They are among the most mobile people in the world. Migrations occurred in the early years of the Conquest when many Indians fled the oppressive rule of the Spanish and Portuguese. Many Indians moved deeper into the interior of the continent only to be pursued by slave-seeking expeditions (*bandeiras*) of the so-called *bandeirantes* of São Paulo. Between the Conquest and the twentieth century, migrations have resulted from the opening of new mines in countries such as Mexico and Peru, where mining was important to pre-

population (1970)

Figures show the total population and the density (average number of persons per square mile) for each country.

U. S. A.

MEXICO
50,700,000
(64.2)

BR. HONDURAS
120,000 (13.5)

CUBA
8,400,000
(180)

HAITI
5,200,000
(480)

DOMINICAN REPUBLIC
4,300,000 (208)

GUATEMALA
5,100,000 (123)

PUERTO RICO
2,800,000 (815)

EL SALVADOR
3,400,000 (399)

HONDURAS
2,700,000 (66)

JAMAICA
2,000,000
(445)

BARBADOS
300,000 (1.517)

PANAMA
1,500,000 (48)

TRINIDAD & TOBAGO
1,100,000 (527)

NICARAGUA
2,000,000
(37)

COSTA RICA
1,800,000
(82)

VENEZUELA
10,800,000
(28)

GUYANA
700,000 (8.1)

SURINAM
389,000 (7)

COLOMBIA
21,400,000
(46.5)

FRENCH GUIANA
40,000 (1.14)

ECUADOR
6,100,000
(54)

PERU
13,600,000
(26.5)

BRAZIL
93,000,000
(27.6)

CHILE
9,800,000
(32)

BOLIVIA
4,600,000
(11.3)

PARAGUAY
2,400,000
(15)

ARGENTINA
24,300,000
(22.4)

URUGUAY
2,900,000
(40)

GENERAL DISTRIBUTION OF THE POPULATION

Population in Latin America (*Data from the Population Reference Bureau, Inc., and* The New York Times Almanac, 1971.)

47

Columbian societies, and in Brazil, where a new source of wealth was created with the discovery of gold deposits near Ouro Preto in the 1690s. The extension of sugar plantations along Northeast Brazil and within the Antilles in the colonial period was accompanied by a migration of people. Subsequent crop heydays in tobacco, coffee, and rubber have also brought their rush of workers.

In recent decades, mass migrations have occurred as people searched for greater economic opportunity. The notorious poverty areas of Northeast Brazil have always exported people to southern Brazil. The strength and direction of these migrations have shifted with time and with changing economic fortunes in the rest of the country, but, in general, they have been northeast-to-south movements. In southern Brazil, there has also been a general westerly movement of people in search of new forested lands which could be turned into coffee *fazendas.* The *marcha para o oeste* has progressed to the extent that intensive commercial production of rice is now carried on in interior Goias.

Pioneer movements are occurring on a small scale in lowland Bolivia and Peru where the Indian people of the *altiplano* are being encouraged to move eastward into the *Oriente* of Bolivia and into the *montaña* piedmont area east of the Andes in Peru. Another pioneer activity of a very different nature is occurring in Venezuela, where an industrial "Ruhr" has been established in a formerly empty area, the Orinoco complex at Santo Thomé de Guyana.

Some of the migrations have been the result of government planning, with the government providing tax or land incentives to encourage people to move, but this has been no guarantee of success. Most migrations have been spontaneous. For the most part, about half of all the urban growth of cities (i.e., about 3 out of 6 percent) is the result of inward migration from small towns and rural areas. Very few people move directly from the farm to the national capital. Still, the movement to more promising rural areas has continued and even accelerated since World War II, but it has by no means begun to match the magnitude of the rural-to-urban push.

Patterns of Urbanization

Cities in Latin America are growing at fantastic rates. Many of the largest cities are increasing their population by 5–6 percent each year. Why is this growth happening? Where do the people come from? What do they do when they get to the cities?

It must be understood that Latin America, in common with other developing areas around the world, is experiencing the transformation from a traditional semifeudal society to an open industrial society where mass production and consumption of goods tend to provide jobs, raise real income levels and hopefully, produce further democratization in the social and political, as well as economic realms. Greater individual prosperity tends to bring greater personal independence. Present-day Latin America, however, operates in both the traditional and modern contexts.

The cities represent the mid-twentieth century: they point the direction in which most of society would like to move. The rural areas, as yet far removed from the modernizing influences of industrialization, still operate in the same way they operated in the eighteenth and nineteenth centuries. Landless peasants, who work for daily wages of fifty cents and who do not own anything except their clothes and a few utensils, have heard of the marvels of city life. For many years a weekly bus filled with migrants has left Fortaleza, Ceara, in Northeast Brazil for São Paulo. People who do not have enough money for the bus fare ride in the backs of trucks. Some people even walk the entire distance carrying their personal belongings on their backs and their infants in their arms. Many of them have left the predictable, grinding poverty of rural areas for the unpredictable city life where they sometimes find success or, frequently, more poverty.

Despite the number of new industries that have been established in the cities, there are still insufficient jobs for all the people looking for work. Many of them return to their home towns; others even commute. There are people in Northeast Brazil who plant a maize crop at the beginning of the February-March rainy season, travel to Rio or São Paulo to work in a factory for four or five months, and then return home to harvest the crop and be with their families.

For many Latin Americans, the move to the city does not improve their own lives, but the lives of their children, who will have access to schools, medical help, and other services which the city provides. Parents may continue to work as unskilled laborers—sweeping streets, washing cars, selling lottery tickets, or washing clothes—while, hopefully, their children may attend school and learn some skill. Most migrants are lucky if they can secure even a low paying job as a domestic servant or menial laborer. As in all developing countries, there is a glut of unskilled labor on the market and a great scarcity of skilled labor. The influx of unskilled workers into the cities of Belo Horizonte, Rio, São Paulo, Curitiba, Porto Alegre, has provided the manpower with which to build the rapidly growing metropolises. Brazil's new capital, Brasilia, for instance, was built largely by workers who migrated from Minas Gerais, Goiás, and the Northeast of Brazil.

The capital cities of Latin America also tend to be the most densely populated. Only in Ecuador and Brazil are the largest cities not the capital. Over the past hundred years, the percentage of the total population residing in the capital city of each country has risen. This means that Latin America is becoming more and more a place of city dwellers. Argentina and Uruguay exhibit this concentration of population to an unusual degree. Over one-third of Argentina's population lives in greater Buenos Aires; almost half of all Uruguayans live in and around Montevideo.

Urban slums are a natural result of such rapid urbanization. The people who migrate to the cities usually arrive with very little money, if any. They may move in with relatives, but more commonly they put together a shack on the outskirts of town and become squatters on unoccupied land (*favelas* in Brazil, *barriadas* in Peru). From there they attempt to find work.

There are various economic levels among urban slums. There are middle-class, upper lower-class, lower middle-class, and lower lower-class *favelas*. Some of the better *favelas* are regarded as quite comfortable dwelling places. Most, however, have a shocking lack of running water, sewers, and electricity. Culturally, the *favelas* are subcities within the large city; they have their own small commercial districts, their own sociological grouping, and except for their location and physical appearance, are quite like any other subdivision of the city.

It was formerly believed that people who flocked into the cities came from outright rural areas. Recent research about Recife, however, has indicated that the great majority of newcomers have moved in from nearby areas or from smaller cities in the interior; very few, in fact, came directly from the farm to the city.[2]

Some large cities, such as Quito (Ecuador) and Salvador (Brazil), are growing more slowly than other cities because of less economic opportunity, i.e., fewer jobs. A more significant distinction appears with smaller cities and towns. In the interior of Northeast Brazil, for instance, towns with less than forty or fifty thousand people experience difficulty in expanding. They tend to remain stagnant, whereas towns with more than forty thousand people tend to attract an increasing diversity of functions. This diversity of urban functions, in turn, attracts the people. Functional diversity is one way of distinguishing "urban" from "rural" communities:

The fact that Minas Velhas [fictitious name for a former county seat in backland Brazil] was founded as a mining town, from the outset a food-consuming rather than a food-producing community, an administrative, religious and educational center, profoundly different from the rural villages, is apparently of greater account in determining its urban characteristics than its size or proximity to a metropolis. If Minas Velhas is at all typical of the many hundred small Brazilian county seats, the mere size of interior settlements or their distance from the coast is not a reliable index of the degree of urbanization.[3]

[2] Levy Cruz, "Caracterização Social," *As Migrações para o Recife* (Recife, 1961–62), p. 158.
[3] Marvin Harris, *Town and Country in Brazil* (Columbia University Press, 1956), p. 277.

CHAPTER 6

economic activities

Subsistence Economic Activities: Hunting, Gathering, and Fishing

Latin America possibly encompasses a more complete range of economic and technical activities than exists anywhere else in the world, from Stone Age hunting and gathering to atomic reactors. This is one of the attractions of Latin America: one can step back in time by simply changing one's location. One can return to the seventeenth or eighteenth centuries in some towns and to a pre-historic era in the remote vastness of the interior of South America and Central America, where it seems as though Cortes and Pizarro had never set foot in the New World.

The nature and variety of economic activities determine the degree to which individuals can control their lives. Subsistence hunting, fishing, and gathering is the way of life for only a small number of people in Latin America; but the area in which these subsistence activities takes place is very large. These are the areas which no one else wants or can yet use.

These activities, however remote and unreal they may seem to North Americans in the mid-twentieth century, are part of the historical development of mankind. The subsistence activities represent significant advances even as the invention of language, tools, weapons, and cooking did for prehistoric man.

According to Preston E. James, there have been three periods of fundamental revolutionary change in human history:

1. the Agricultural Revolution, occurring around 8000 B.C. in Southwest Asia and East Africa, during which a number of plants and animals were first domesticated.

2. the Industrial Revolution, occurring in the late eighteenth century in the lands bordering the North Sea, during which the innovation of power-driven machinery added to man's collection of devices, easing his burdens of living and aiding his attempts to build a higher civilization.
3. the Democratic Revolution occurring contemporaneously with the beginnings of industrialization, which brought the ideas of participatory democracy to bear upon political states.[1]

All over the world today, developing nations are experiencing the effects of their own industrial and democratic revolutions. It is this discordant development which accounts for many political, economic, and social inequalities throughout the world.

Hunting, fishing, and gathering were the daily subsistence activities of the Indian populations of pre-Columbian America, and they are also the present way of life for about 100,000 Indians of Brazil living in the remote areas of Mato Grosso, Goiás, and Amazonas today. Other small tribes, such as the Lacandones in Chiapas, Mexico, are people who still live mainly by these means.

Shifting agriculture, the so-called slash and burn system, represents a tremendous advance over hunting and gathering because it means that the individual has control over his source of food supply. With shifting agriculture, a plot of land is cleared, the brush is burned at the end of the dry season, and the ground is planted with crops such as maize, beans, manioc. After several years, when the soils become exhausted and the crop yields have fallen, the field is abandoned, another area cleared, and the cycle is repeated.

Shifting agriculture is known by many names around the world and, in Latin America, it has several names: *roça* agriculture in Brazil, *milpa* or *canuco* in Mexico. Although there are slight variations in the slash and burn system of shifting cultivation, the dominant characteristics remain as described above.

In Latin America, of course, some people have combined agriculture with hunting and gathering. Even today one can observe backland farmers walking to their farm plots with shotguns over their shoulders in the hope that they might shoot a bird or other small animal for supper.

Commercial Economic Activities

We have just looked at some examples of the kinds of activities in which people engage to insure survival for themselves and their families. In this system, there is not enough surplus to sell. People try to produce only what is required for their family's basic needs. With commercial economic activities, we begin to examine the economics of large-scale operations.

The first commercial enterprises in the New World were gold mining and the extraction of dyewoods. As early as the 1520s sugarcane

[1] Preston E. James, *One World Divided* (Blaisdell Publishing Co., 1964), pp. 15–31.

plantations were established along the coast of Northeast Brazil. Soon a number of different activities were begun in those areas best suited to them. Fiber crops, such as cotton in Mexico, Peru, and Brazil, jute in the Amazon, and henequen in Yucatán, brought income to Latin America and to Spain and Portugal during the colonial period. Coffee plantations became profitable enterprises during the nineteenth and twentieth centuries in most Central American countries and on the well-drained slopes of tropical South America. Other plantation products include cacao, bananas, and rubber. Rubber planatations, however, were less successful in the New World than in Malaya.

Commercial grain farming became more prevalent in the nineteenth century. Wheat and alfalfa were grown on the Humid Pampa and exported to European markets at that time. Commercial farming today is evidenced by the market gardens and trench farms which surround most cities of Latin America.

Despite the variety of commercial activities, one striking fact remains: the amount of actual cultivated land is only two percent of the entire area of Latin America. This means that most of the land is unused, and, moreover, that most of the land that is used is used inefficiently. The existence of large tracts of land, virtually tax-free, means that landowners do not have to be efficient in their use of land resources. Cost-benefit studies and systems analyses are still not a part of the Latin American agricultural picture.

One example of the inefficiency of land use is the way some cattle are raised. With the exception of ranchers in Argentina, Uruguay, and a few enlightened cattle raisers in other countries, most cattle raising is extensive and not intensive. The breeds are not sufficiently selected; the forage upon which the animals feed is not controlled to produce quality beef. In Brazil, for example, beef cattle are driven as much as several hundred miles to market, and are owned by three or four different *fazendeiros* during the fattening period. By the time these animals arrive at the slaughterhouse, the quality of their beef has dropped. Moreover, the meat is expensive since so many middlemen have taken a profit at each stage of the operation.[2]

In Argentina the system of beef supply attempts to provide quality meat. The animals tend to be fattened on one property until sent to the slaughterhouse. There is an attempt to adapt the quality of the meat to the preferences of the market.

There are many extractive industries for which Latin America is noted. The colonial period witnessed the extraction of gold and silver and of dyewoods. Subsequent centuries have witnessed the discovery of oil and the opening up of other kinds of mines which yielded copper, lead, zinc, and diamonds. Brazilwood gathering yielded to forestry. One of the few commercial activities which remote areas of the Amazon Basin and Middle America can support is the extraction of hardwoods for the making of quality furniture and high-quality wood veneer products.

[2] Kempton E. Webb, *A Geography of Food Supply in Central Minas Gerais* (National Academy of Sciences, National Research Council, 1959), p. 55.

Fishing is an extractive industry which enjoys an uneven success. Peru has made fishing profitable with its development of an anchovy fish meal industry in the 1960s. Yet, in Brazil, where so many people live close to the seashore, it is ironic that the fishing industry is as yet undeveloped. Although people who live near the sea consume a great deal of seafood, the facilities for storing and shipping fish are very limited. Very little fresh fish is available at any distance from the beaches. Along the coast of Northeast Brazil, from Salvador to Fortaleza, fishermen still go out in the colorful, picturesque *jangada* sailing rafts. For all its picturesqueness, *jangada* fishing is not only extremely inefficient, it is also very dangerous. Research is now underway to develop an efficient modern fishing industry on the coast of Northeast Brazil. This will necessarily involve modernization of boats and methods of bulk handling, storage, and shipping.

Industrialization, however, creates grave social and economic problems, especially the question of what to do with the people who will be put out of work by automation. When modern industrial countries like the United States cannot solve the problem of employment of unskilled workers, the outlook for Latin America is not encouraging.

Patterns of Industry and Manufacturing

The industrial development of Latin America reflects the mercantile heritage of Spain and Portugal. Industry in Latin America has been closely associated with urban areas, even in the colonial periods. Although Spain and Portugal intended to keep their colonies dependent on their respective mother countries for manufactured goods, it was inevitable that some light industry would arise to meet local needs for food, furniture, soap, etc. The first industry in Latin America which showed the impact of the Industrial Revolution was textiles, and it was largely British technology and capital which launched these mid-nineteenth century ventures in Brazil, Mexico, and Argentina.

Until recently, however, prestige still accrued to people who owned land, and not to those who owned factories. The economic philosophies evidenced in modern cities such as Mexico City, Buenos Aires, São Paulo, and Caracas, are identical to any modern industrial city in Western Europe or North America. Industrial development in Latin America has principally taken place around the large cities, reinforcing the primacy of capital cities. Diversification of industry since World War II has succeeded in the substitution of domestically made good for imported ones, in items such as refrigerators, radios, television sets, cars, and trucks.

Most of the industry of Latin America is light, not heavy, industry. There is a certain amount of iron and steel production but its magnitude is not comparable to that of the leading industrial nations. This combination of light industry, the large-scale extraction industry, and exportation of raw materials has characterized Latin America's economic life for over a hundred years. Latin America has lacked the disposition and encouragement to save in order to accumulate capital for industrial production. Since World War II, however, Brazil, Mexico, Venezuela, Argentina, and Colombia have fostered their own industrial growth, but often with foreign financing.

Before World War II most manufacturing was in food and beverage processing and clothing manufacture. Since 1945 the pattern has become more diversified, especially in iron and steel manufacturing. Some countries, like Brazil, manufacture television sets, refrigerators, telephones, automobiles, and more recently, ships and machine tools. Exporting these manufactured items improves the balance of trade for the Latin American exporter country. The manufacturers will also play a significant role in any developments which the LAFTA (Latin American Free Trade Area) will experience.

Productivity is the key to an industrial economy and automation is the key to productivity. In Latin America, however, most manufacturing plants still have an unusually large labor force, even in such an automated industry as beverage bottling. Of course, the lack of suitable transportation facilities tends to protect an inefficient manufacturer in the backlands from unfavorable competition with a superior producer from the cities. As roads improve, this closed market situation in the remote areas will yield to a more open competitive market system.

CHAPTER 7 *transportation and communication*

Pre-Industrial Modes of Transportation

The distinguishing characteristic of pre-industrial communication and transportation is that mechanical energy had not yet become an integral part of man's systems for moving himself and his goods. In many areas of Latin America, rudimentary communications still persist. The lines of communication in any era comprise the lifelines over which ideas as well as people and goods circulate. In pre-nineteenth century Latin America, the pack trails and rugged coach roads represented, no less than the modern highways and airline routes of today, a reaching-out to combat the isolation and remoteness which characterizes so many areas of Latin America.

It may be helpful to visualize a cross section in which different modes of transportation are represented as horizontal layers. The lowermost layer corresponds to transportation by burro or mule. The next layer represents wheeled transportation (coaches and wagons) of the pre-industrial era. Superimposed upon that would come railroad transportation, followed by the motor truck and automobile, and finally, by the airplane. This many-layered "sandwich" represents the different means of communication and transportation extending over Latin America. In many areas, all five types are found in the same place; in remoter places, there may be only two or three. Where there exists a paucity of modern transportation, only the animal-drawn conveyances and the airplane are available, with no sign of highway or railroad facilities. Especially in isolated mountainous areas where the amount of goods produced does not warrant vast investments in roads and railroads, these so-called primitive transportation modes are still the most appropriate means of moving people and goods from place to place.

Unlike North America, Latin America does not have an integrated system of transportation. There are broad areas where only primitive transportation exists. In a context of such limited facilities, there is little competition among available carriers. Transportation costs, therefore, are relatively high. There are few, if any, economies of scale which are capable of moving large quantities of goods over long distances at very low per-unit rates, as is characteristic of an industrialized competitive society. For example, fresh vegetables and fruits destined for the Fortaleza markets in Ceará, Brazil come from a mountainous zone called Maranguape, where the various food commodities are carried on the backs of animals (burros and horses) some five kilometers to a point where a truck transports them thirty kilometers to the city. The cost of moving the commodities five kilometers is five times the cost of the truck transport to Fortaleza, and yet the distance the animals walk is only a fifth of the trucking distance.[1]

In the pre-Conquest period, there were no beasts of burden at all, except the llama which could carry only loads up to ninety pounds. Human porters were the main means of transporting goods. Needless to say, mostly small items were transported, and this limitation appears to have had a stabilizing effect upon the population distribution during that period. With the Conquest came horses, mules, burros, and oxen—domesticated animals which could be put to work. The oxcart is still a common feature of the rural landscape in many parts of Latin America. A typical noontime scene in a village *praça* of Northeast Brazil usually includes fifteen or twenty tethered horses and a solitary Jeep sharing the shady area. This is an indication of the relative importance of animal transportation in the remote areas. The long pack trains of mules, burros, and horses comprised the lifelines of supply to the Andean mines of Peru and Bolivia as did the pack trains which lead from São Paulo and the *campos* of Uruguay and Rio Grande do Sul toward the gold mines of Minas Gerais and as far north as Bahia.

During the colonial period, when the Europeans introduced horses and cattle into the cultural landscape, there developed a whole leather-craft culture to provide the accessories associated with animal transport. One Brazilian geographer, Aroldo de Azevedo, has written of the "leather cycle" in Brazilian history since this material was so universally used. Not only were reins, harnesses, saddles, and other horse trappings made of leather, but also chairs, beds, shipping containers, trunks, and clothing. One gets the impression that leather occupied as central a place in everyday colonial life as iron and steel do in our present daily life.

Slopes were not a significant problem to pack trains but they were to railroads which began to be built in the middle of the nineteenth century. Recent research done by Richard Momsen [2] mentions the various "route ways" over the Sierra do Mar, the steep escarpment back of Rio

---

[1] Kempton E. Webb, *Suprimento de Generos Alimenticios Para a Cidade de Fortaleza* (Banco do Nordeste do Brazil, 1957).

[2] Richard Momsen, "Routes over the Serra do Mar," *Revista Geografica*, vol. 32 (1963), 5–167.

Noontime traffic in the praça *of a small town in the interior of Ceará, Brazil.
(This could just as easily be a view of eighteenth-century Brazil!)*

and Santos, and the fact that early pack trails generally sought the most
direct route; they would, if necessary, traverse extremely steep slopes
to reduce distances and travel time. Railroad construction, and later,
highway construction, required more gradual slopes, and many of the
old pack trails had to be abandoned because they were too steep.

There are some areas of Latin America, especially in Guatemala
and southern Mexico, where people still carry loads on their heads or
with tumplines, or headbands, another carryover from pre-Columbian
times. In Brazil and throughout much of the Caribbean area today, people
carry surprisingly heavy loads on their heads.

Primitive forms of transportation still exist in areas where essentially subsistence economic activities are practiced. Obviously, to maintain machinery, such as a tractor or truck, in a remote area poses a
serious problem regarding repairs and replacement of worn parts. These
pre-industrial modes of transportation, picturesque in photographs and
tourist brochures, are still very much a part of everyday life in the remote areas all over Latin America. It is in this realm of transportation that
the industrial way of life usually makes its earliest and strongest impact.

Waterways, Railroads, and Roads

Transport by sea and inland waterways was the precursor of rail
transport. The use of inland waterways in Latin America has suffered

from several inherent drawbacks. Since most of the navigable streams are located in sparsely populated areas which have low productivity, they serve these areas only in limited ways. Many of the larger rivers have rapids in their lower portions; many have fluctuating regimes in which the difference between high and low stages of the river limits the period of navigability to but a few months of the year. The inland waterways suffer from the same limitations as the railroad since both require a fixed and limited right of way and since development for both involves a large investment in equipment.

Coastwise shipping has always been important within Latin America. During the colonial period the residents of Latin America and those who traveled there considered overland transportation only as a last resort. Despite its precarious nature at this time, voyagers preferred the uncertainties and risks of sea travel to the very real hardship and endurance tests of overland travel by coach. To this day there are still more potholed roads than paved roads in Latin America, as any well-traveled visitor will attest.

Most of the larger cities were located on or near the coast, and thus formed a linear pattern of trade centers convenient to coastwise shipping routes. Ports formed some of the earliest nuclei of settlement, and they often became dominant and primate cities. One has only to list the cities of Salvador (Bahia, the first capital of Brazil 1549–1763), Rio de Janeiro (the second capital of Brazil, 1763–1960), Montevideo, Buenos Aires, Lima, Guayaquil, Panama, Havana, and Santo Domingo, to appreciate the coincidence between port and primate city. The existence of this linear arrangement of large cities tended to reinforce the coastwise shipping and transportation patterns until well into this century. It is only since World War II that significant new and different lines of penetration by highways have been laid out.

The earliest railroads in Latin America were built in the period following 1850, with very few additional lines being added after 1930. It is important to note that the primary reason for the construction of railroads was not to serve population centers but rather to move commercial crops and raw materials from their remote interior sources to ports from which they could be shipped abroad, usually to North America or Western Europe. The map on p. 60 indicates this general pattern of linking hinterland with ports. Only in a few instances do railroads run parallel to the coast, connecting the coastal population centers.

A great problem of railroads in Latin America is that they do not form an integrated system. Many railroads are made up of single track lines with occasional spurs. Moreover, different gauges of track width are found even within a single country, such as Brazil, a factor which further complicates the establishment of through service.

True railway networks exist in only a few areas of Latin America: Central Mexico, the Humid Pampa of Argentina (probably the best example of a dense network of railway lines and service), southern Brazil (focusing upon São Paulo), and finally the thin networks operating in parts of Peru, Uruguay, and Colombia.

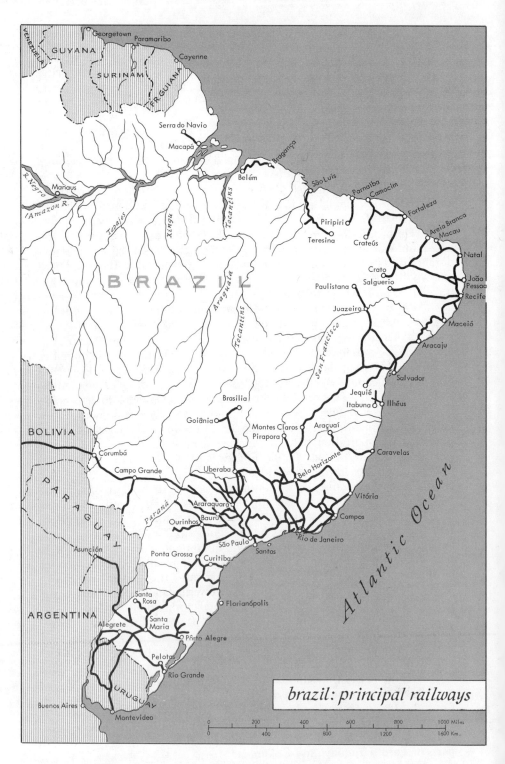

brazil: principal railways

The Humid Pampa of Argentina has often been pointed out as an example of an area where the railroads were the principal means of attracting population and extending settlement patterns during the nineteenth century. However, recent research indicates that the formative stages of commercial agriculture on the Humid Pampa began around 1860 and preceded the building of the first railroads. It was in fact, the very isolation of those early wheat growing areas of Santa Fé province which provided the favorable conditions under which to innovate and develop a commercial agriculture.[3] Of course, in subsequent years railroads did stimulate and benefit not only commercial farming but also modernization of the beef production industry.

The earliest highways were nothing more than improved coach roads over which people attempted to drive automobiles. It is difficult to imagine that Latin America lacked motor roads and highways as recently as 1930 and 1940. The traffic on whatever roads existed was mainly trucks and some buses, and it was not until after World War II that passenger automobiles traveled on roads outside of the major cities. For a person to attempt to take a cross country automobile trip before or even immediately following World War II was a true adventure. There were few gas stations between towns, and even fewer repair shops; there were hazards of all types which might befall the travelers of those narrow, rutted roads.

One outstanding development which has captured the imagination of many people is the Inter-American Highway. This is actually a series of interlinking national highways extending all the way from Alaska, through Canada, the United States, Mexico, and Central America, to just south of the Panama Canal. A gap exists between Panama and Colombia, but the South American segment makes it possible for a person to drive all the way from easternmost Venezuela through Colombia, Ecuador, and Peru, to Tierra del Fuego of southernmost South America. This is a symbolic highway; it is a diplomatic gesture; mostly financed by the United States, symbolizing the linking together of all the American Republics. The Inter-American Highway is not a great avenue of commerce from one end of Latin America to the other, but rather, a road which provides transportation usually within each country. Only the occasional traveler actually uses the road as a truly inter-American travel corridor.

Modern Roads and Airlines

The period following 1945 and, even more strikingly, since 1955, has been a time of extensive road building projects in practically all countries of Latin America. Most modern roads differ from earlier ones in that they are built for higher speeds and heavier use. Most of the new roads are not only all-weather roads, but many are paved at the time of construction. The sudden acceleration of road building after 1955 occurred be-

[3] Rolf Stemberg, "Farms and Farmers in an Estanceros World" (Unpublished Doctoral thesis, Syracuse University, 1971).

cause highways were then acknowledged as profound agents of economic and social development. In Mexico, the excellent paved highways extending northward from Mexico City to the United States border have been an economic lifeline over which a million tourists come every year. They spend enough money to account for most of the foreign exchange earnings of Mexico. In this way, Mexico benefits directly from its physical proximity to the United States.

An interesting development is occurring in the Andean countries: a new Marginal Highway is being planned to extend from north to south, thus linking the Andean countries east of the mountains. It would run parallel to the Inter-American highway but would be located between the mountains and the lowland rainforest. This is an outstanding development because it pioneers road building in an area where there are no roads of a north-south orientation. It will provide, moreover, the second side to which east-west crossroads can link. In other words, it is the beginning of a latticework of roads over the Andean area.

Brazil has undertaken the most ambitious road-building program since the middle 1950s. The new roads have been extended to the new capital of Brasilia and beyond to Belém, and highways are now being extended from Brasilia to Porto Velho, ultimately to link up with Pucallpa and the Peruvian trans-Andean road. There is also a proposed road from Brasilia to Bogotá via Manaus and a trans-Amazon highway extending from east to west through the Amazon Basin. These are bold plans which even ten years ago seemed preposterous, but the success of former highways has justified the investment for new ones. The provision of all-weather roads guarantees cities a steady incoming stream of needed goods and farmers a competitive market for their crops, enabling them to keep their land in production. All-weather roads guarantee that the person in the backlands will be able to buy the same manufactured items at competitive costs that his city-dwelling relatives enjoy. Brazil, probably more than any other Latin American country, exhibits a national highway planning strategy which involves the amoebalike expansion of the highway network to the outermost reaches of the national territory. The aim, of course, is to incorporate those remote areas of the Amazon and the extreme west of Brazil so that they may contribute to the economic life of the country.[4] Truck transport, though high priced, is preferred by many people to rail transport. Truck transportation is generally faster (for distances under 500 miles) and is more reliable with less loss and spoilage of produce. These factors are considered by most people to be well worth the added cost of shipping by truck rather than by rail.

Some people are surprised to learn that Latin America is well served by frequent and widely ranging airplane service, for many of us tend to equate airline traffic with an advanced stage of economic development. The fact is that the airplane is uniquely suited to developing countries because, outside of the initial investment in aircraft, airports, and main-

[4] Kempton E. Webb, "The Geography of Brazil's Modernization and Implications for the Years 1980 and 2000 A.D.," in *The Shaping of Modern Brazil*, ed. Eric Baklanoff (Louisiana State University Press, 1969), pp. 142–56.

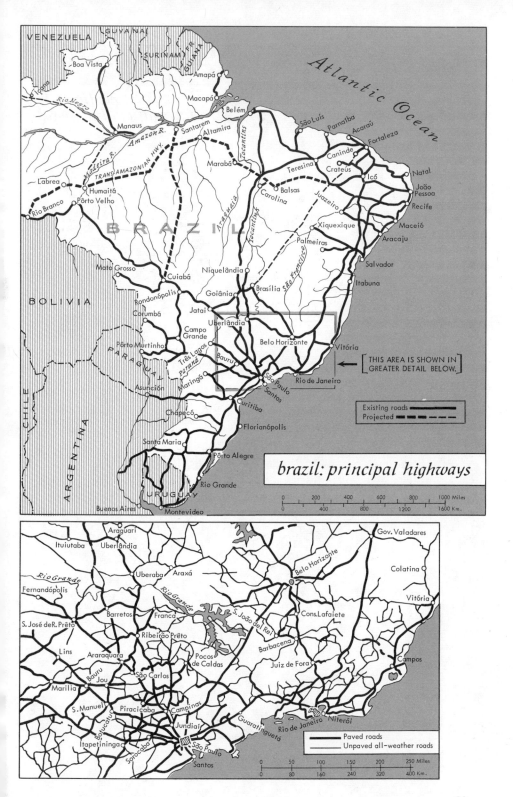

brazil: principal highways

Existing roads
Projected

THIS AREA IS SHOWN IN
GREATER DETAIL BELOW.

0	200	400	600	800	1000 Miles
0	400	800	1200	1600 Km.	

Paved roads
Unpaved all-weather roads

0	50	100	150	200	250 Miles
0	80	160	240	320	400 Km.

brazil: domestic and
international airways

tenance facilities, only a minimum of investment is required. The Amazon Basin and the remote parts of Middle America are crisscrossed by airline routes, and it is the very absence of alternative means of surface communication which guarantees traffic for the airlines. For this reason, airlines are very important in remote areas not only as carriers of passengers and low-bulk–high-value items, but also as carriers of ordinary freight and foodstuffs.

The increasing use of airplanes as freight carriers is recognition of the fact that time is money, and that a manufacturer's service to his clients and customers involves the prompt delivery of ordered items. Air freight provides that means.

The map of airline services of Brazil shown here is representative of the air service within much of Latin America. How can the revenues from air service in extremely remote areas of western and northern Brazil possibly pay for the services provided? Air fares are very low per kilometer flown, and the volume and frequency of travel is not high. In fact, the air fares in the remoter areas are subsidized by the Brazilian government.

Let us picture an imaginary line connecting Belem, Brasilia, and Porto Alegre, dividing eastern Brazil from western Brazil. The air traffic east of that line generally pays its own way, whereas the costs of air travel west of that line are not covered by revenues from fares and freight fees. This illustrates how governments can help airlines and thereby subsidize development in those areas. It is hoped that the small interior communities will grow and become sufficiently productive to justify the construction of alternative means of transportation. In the meantime, relatively inexpensive air fares allow those communities to benefit from contacts with the more densely settled areas of the country. In air travel, as with rail and highway transportation, economies of scale have tended to bring unit costs down to more competitive levels.

CHAPTER **8** *andean america*

The Andes are a complex system, not a simple, single range of mountains. In Peru and Bolivia they form the broad altiplano which is surmounted by snowcapped peaks, and in Bolivia they are almost 400 miles wide. In Ecuador the Andes are made up of a north-south corridor flanked by two imposing rows of volcanoes. In Colombia they form three distinct *cordilleras* or ranges, the easternmost of which crosses into Venezuela where it assumes an east-west trend, extending as far east as the island of Trinidad.

Both the driest and the wettest places in Latin America are found in the Andes: the Atacama Desert, and the western flank zone of the Colombian Chocó region, where the town of Quibdo registers 415 inches of rain per year. Not only do different ranges separate various areas within one country, as in Ecuador, but there are also separate basins within the large intermontane corridor. Each basin in the Indian areas of highland South America (essentially Ecuador, Peru, and Bolivia) has its own cultural flavor, sometimes quite distinct from those of its neighboring regions.

Surprisingly, there is very little contact or commerce between the countries through which the Andes extend. Because of the fairly similar physical attributes of each of these countries, one might think that there would be much economic and cultural exchange. The Andes, however, pose a formidable barrier of transportation costs and high tariffs to both inter- and intranational communication.

The varying significance of this mountain system is seen clearly in the differences in patterns of habitation from one region to another. In Venezuela, the peaks between 12,000 and 15,000 feet are uninhabited, yet it is precisely within this altitude range in the altiplano of Peru and

Above: *Indian fiesta celebrants outside a church in Pisac, Peru. These are Quechua-speaking peoples who practice intensive agriculture on terraces and bottomland prepared by their Inca ancestors. Below: Aymara Indian women at a street market in La Paz, Bolivia.*

Bolivia that large numbers of people live. In Chile, on the other hand, the highest areas are empty of people. These differences can also be related to the ethnic make-up of the populations. In Venezuela and Colombia, where the people are largely mestizo, population is densest at middle and middle-lower elevations. In Ecuador, Peru, and Bolivia, the population is largely Indian on the highlands and mestizo at lower elevations. The largely European population of Chile is concentrated at the lowest elevations.

In many ways, these present-day patterns echo the route of the European conquerors and the accompanying withdrawal of the native population. The Andes region was the very first area in South America penetrated by the Spaniards (as shown in the map on p. 22). The earliest settlements followed a route from the Caribbean across the isthmus of Panama and southward along the west coast to Ecuador and Peru. The line of penetration then headed toward the Inca realms, the gold and silver mines of highland Peru and Bolivia, and then on to northwestern Argentina. The penetration and effective settlement of the eastern side of the Andes and the interior of South America came at a later time.

Peru: The Inca Heartland

The altiplano portion of the central Andes of Peru (and Bolivia) was the core of the Inca Empire and the flower of pre-Columbian culture within South America. We have already become acquainted with some of the pre-Conquest and immediate post-Conquest aspects of Peru in the introductory chapter of this book. Let us now look more closely at this area.

The country of Peru can be divided into three physical regions: (*1*) the *costa,* or coastal zone; (*2*) the *sierra,* meaning the Andes; and (*3*) the *montaña,* or forested lands of the eastern Andean slopes and Amazon lowland. Each of these zones has its own specific assemblage of physical characteristics which distinguishes it from adjacent regions.

The *costa* is part of that great dry zone extending from southwesternmost Ecuador in a belt of varying width southward into northern Chile. This almost uniformly dry zone actually crosses the Andes diagonally from northwest to southeast reaching all the way to Patagonia. The key to habitability along the *costa,* as in all deserts, is the availability of water. The almost negligible amount of rainfall in the area is counteracted only by the glacier-fed streams flowing as exotic rivers westward toward the coast from the Andes. Many of the river valleys have been adapted to irrigation, and these ribbons of green are the only signs of life in an otherwise barren and beige wasteland.

The *sierra* of Peru has a distinct ecology which might appear hostile to human habitation; yet this was the very culture hearth of the Inca Empire. It is an area in which the Indians of the pre-Conquest period formed highly effective working relationships with their soil, plant, and water resources. The altiplano surface varies from 11,000 to 14,000 feet elevation, and is a late mature uplifted erosion surface across which

Lake "Huacachina" in Ica, Peru   (Courtesy of the Embassy of Peru).

streams meander rather sluggishly before plunging down the precipitous eastern flanks of the Andes. Research done among the Indians living at this high altitude in a rarefied atmosphere shows that the lung capacity of the altiplano inhabitants is significantly larger than that of the coastal peoples. The traveler who visits the Andean area from lower elevations notices immediately the effect: he feels weak, out of breath, and has difficulty sleeping because he must breathe more quickly in order to absorb sufficient oxygen.

Only the hardiest plants, such as barley and potatoes, are found at the higher elevations; potatoes are grown as high as 14,500 feet. *Quinoa* is another high altitude grain plant. Around the shores of Lake Titicaca, where one of the densest rural populations of Latin America is found, the moderating effects of the water body limit the daily, as well as seasonal, temperature extremes, thus permitting the cultivations of crops, such as maize, which otherwise grow only at lower elevations.

The *montaña* is an area of low population, very high rainfall, dense vegetation, and steep slopes. The Inca Empire only extended into this region to establish outpost fortifications, such as Macchu Picchu, overlooking the Urubamba River. The rainfall averages over 100 inches yearly in many places and the temperatures hover in the 80s at the lowermost elevations.

PRE-CONQUEST PERU.   The Inca Empire was the culminating point of higher culture in South America—the last chapter in a history of cultural evolution which extended for almost 4000 years before the coming of

The ruins of Tiahuanaco, which date back to the time of Christ, near Guaqui on the Bolivian shore of Lake Titicaca. The frequent seismic activity in the Andean zone has altered the original arrangement of stones.

the Spaniards. The Inca Empire, with its seat in Cuzco, reached as far north as the present southern border of Colombia and as far south as northeastern Argentina and northern Chile.

One of the precursors of the Inca Empire was the early Tiahuanaco civilization with its seat just south of Lake Titicaca in present-day Bolivia. The ruins at Tiahuanaco can be seen today, and, while they are not as extensive or monumental as those of later Inca structures, such as Macchu Picchu, they are almost more impressive because of their much greater antiquity and the fact that they were built at a time when people had even less technology than the Incas had.

The Inca Empire flourished between the twelfth and fifteenth centuries A.D. The Incas succeeded in dominating several other well developed Indian areas. Both the victors and the vanquished were acculturated through the mutual adoption of superior aspects of each other's cultures. The Incas even resettled large segments of population in order to more successfully integrate the conquered peoples into the Inca system. The Incas succeeded in imposing, for the first time, a single language (Quechua) over the entire area where formerly there were dozens of different tongues. Some students of pre-Columbian languages think that the Indian languages in parts of Peru were as different from one another as English is from Chinese today.

The Inca regime was a benevolent despotism in that strict but carefully drawn laws governed every aspect of life. All lands and the people on them belonged ultimately to the Inca, yet individuals were permitted the use of the land. The technology of people under the Inca system was limited to the simple hoe and digging-stick agriculture, and they did not have any draft animals with which to pull a plow. Crops were cultivated on mountain slopes made arable by elaborate terracing, irrigation, and the application of fertilizer. Guano (bird excrement) and fish were used for fertilizer, especially along the coast.

The Inca state worked efficiently despite the lack of civil liberties afforded the people. The population received its food supply: fuel and other necessities of life were allocated on the basis of need, and when a change occurred in the size of family through marriage or death, an adjustment was made in the allotment of basic commodities. For a culture which had neither the plow nor the wheel, the Incas attained an amazing degree of development in the realm of crafts and home industries. The Inca craftsmen learned how to fashion elaborate gold and silver ornaments and, even more significant for everyday living, they knew how to make axes and knives from bronze. The variety and beauty of their woven fabrics and the ingenuity of their weaving patterns have not been equaled. The vegetable-dye colors which they used can be observed in museums today and have a brightness that belies their great antiquity. The Inca Empire also boasted skilled technicians in rock quarrying and the construction of monumental buildings. Roads and buildings were built of stone, and it is still a mystery how the people physically handled and fashioned huge blocks of granite to construct such masterpieces as Macchu Picchu.

The accomplishments of the Inca civilization are truly amazing when one considers their lack of beasts of burden and their limited technology which had not even developed the use of the wheel. We may well speculate, wistfully, on what might have happened to the Inca Empire if the Spanish conquerors, with all their European material culture, had been defeated. We may also wonder what the Inca as well as the Aztecs might have become had they had the material and technological accoutrements of European culture (firearms, horses, and wheels, for instance) without the political, social, and economic domination. We shall never know.

THE IMPACT OF SPANISH CULTURE. The main contribution of the Spanish in the New World was the implantation of a radically different material culture on the indigenous peoples—a culture that supported and enforced Spanish political and economic domination. How else but through superior culture and single-mindedness could a few hundred men overthrow an advanced civilization of several million?

The impact of the Europeans on the land and on the people's relationship to the land can be clearly seen in two areas. The first concerns the introduction of new domesticated animals and plants (listed in the Appendix).

Although the pre-Columbian inhabitants had plentiful food plants, they lacked virtually every common farmyard animal. The Spanish brought not only all of the common domesticated animals used for food, but also oxen, horses, and mules, which served as beasts of burden. The New World peoples could finally move themselves and their goods more easily, and their diet became more varied.

The second area was the new notion of individual ownership of land. The Inca system was based on communal ownership; they believed the land was free for all to use, just as we consider the atmosphere public property, free for all to breathe. In establishing individually-owned plantations, the Spanish directly contradicted the Indian culture.

These two cultures were never completely integrated: It is still possible to distinguish between areas of Hispanic and indigenous influence. The Indian culture continues to dominate the altiplano or Highlands, whereas European ways have completely taken over along the coast. A similar distinction can be made between the rural areas, where life continues to follow traditional indigenous patterns, and the cities, which are centers of Spanish culture and twentieth century innovation. The one exception is the coastal area where sugarcane, cotton, and rice are grown; the plantations of this region are culturally European.

CONTEMPORARY PERU.   The economy of Peru today is closely tied to the physical quality of the land and to the peculiarly local cultural definition of resources: physical, human, and technological. The principal areas of commercial agriculture are the irrigated coastal valleys. Here the most efficient means of agriculture are practiced, a striking contrast to the inefficient methods employed in other parts of the country. Although two-thirds of Peru's people are employed in agriculture, many of the products are exported, making it necessary to import substantial quantities of food and other consumer goods. Peru grows and exports a valuable variety of long-staple cotton as well as sugarcane and rice. Cereals are grown at higher elevations, and vegetables, root crops, and fruits are grown at intermediate elevations where the temperature permits.

Most of the livestock activity focuses upon sheep, although wool is not an important exchange earner. Sheep can graze extensively on the high, dry, sparsely covered puna, while cattle are limited to lower elevations. In the 1960s, anchovy fishing has provided large amounts of foreign exchange through the export sales of fish meal.

Minerals are still a significant source of foreign exchange for Peru. Today, however, instead of gold and silver (which are still produced), it is the lead, zinc, copper, and petroleum which account for the greater value.

Lima and Arequipa are the main industrial centers, but their domestic markets are limited by the low purchasing power of most Peruvians. Approximately half of the Peruvian population is composed of altiplano Indians whose consumption is limited largely to subsistence items. These consumers do not generate enough demand to form a market which large national industries could supply.

Peru has a striking geography. Moreover, its history cuts across the great divide between pre- and post-Conquest New World history. The central problem of Peru, as for much of Latin America, is how to weld the diverse and separate areas of different peoples into a coherent, productive whole. There are large segments of the population which have not yet been brought into the effective national life. The great challenge to Peru is how to realize the potential of these vast areas and diverse peoples so that they, as individuals, and the country as a political unit, may progress in a state of mutual benefit.

The Inca fortress city of Macchu Picchu. There are also ruins on the top of nearby Huaynu Picchu in the background.

Bolivia and Ecuador: The Fringes of Inca Influence

BOLIVIA. The precursor of Inca civilization was the early Tiahuanaco culture, which existed on the south shore of Lake Titicaca between 500 B.C. and the beginning of the Christian era. The major present-day Indian group of Bolivia is the Aymara, with only a few Quechua-speaking Indians along the Peruvian altiplano border. The altiplano of Bolivia is drier and less arable than that of Peru. There are many salt lakes and basins of interior drainage which are essentially uninhabited, and it is only in the Yungas area of the eastern Andean slope where any variety of vegetables, coffee, and fruits can be grown.

Bolivia is the only landlocked country of South America, a fact of which Bolivians are very much aware. Bolivia lost its only corridor to the Pacific through the Nitrate War against Chile in 1879. Excepting the dry coastal zone, the physical divisions of Bolivia are the same as those of Peru. The aridity of the Bolivian altiplano more than compensates for the absence of a dry area along the coast, and the moist mesothermal Yungas area, although more densely populated, is more or less equivalent to the *montaña* of Peru.

Lowland Bolivia, namely the Oriente Province, is the second major land category within Bolivia and forms the greater portion of the country; it is also the most sparsely populated part. Most of lowland Bolivia is humid, covered by dense tropical rainforest vegetation. It is the area to which several thousand altiplano Indians have migrated in recent years as part of a government resettlement plan. One of the main reasons for resettlement is the overcrowded living conditions on the altiplano and the sparseness of population in the lowlands to the east. Although there has been some degree of success in relocating the highlanders in Oriente Province, there are many understandable reasons why people do not want to leave familiar surroundings and relatives to move not only to a strange area but also to an entirely different ecology.

Although there is much less commercial agriculture in Bolivia than in Peru, the majority of the people live on the land. For the most part it is a subsistence agriculture which is practiced in Bolivia—the kind of farming not efficient enough to yield marketable surplus and afford the farmer a significant improvement in his standard of living. It is ironic, in a country with such a high proportion of the labor force engaged in agriculture, that the preponderant proportion of Bolivian exports are minerals, mostly tin. But even the mineral resources are unfortunately suffering from the heritage of many years of failure to keep up with expanding technology. The mines are inefficiently operated, and the productivity of labor is low, with the result that the tin produced is among the costliest in the world. In fact, the cost of mining tin is higher than its price in the world market.

Bolivia's revolution in 1952 was supposed to correct some of the economic ills and social problems of the country. As yet, however, progress has been extremely slow.

ECUADOR. Ecuador exhibits the same three dominant types of regions as does Peru: namely the coastlands, the forested lowlands east of mountains, and the Andes.

The Pacific lowlands west of the Andes are only forty to fifty miles wide. At the very foot of the Andes is the humid tropical region with its dense, lush tropical vegetation. The farther west one travels on the narrow coastal plain, the closer one gets to drier and drier conditions. The westernmost area of extreme aridity is simply an extension of the Peruvian coastal desert to the south, and is caused by the extremely stable atmospheric conditions produced by the cold Peru Current. The economic life of Ecuador is centered in the humid coastal area, on the plantations of cacao and bananas. The presence of the Gulf of Guayaquil and the protected anchorage and harbor for shipping has been important in the development of Guayaquil and the coastal lowlands of Ecuador.

The Andes of Ecuador consist of two principal chains, ranging in elevation from 11,000 to 18,000 feet. Between this double line of north-south ramparts lies a series of highland basins between 6000 and 9000 feet, separated from each other by low transverse hills. It is within these small intermontane basins that most of the people of Ecuador live.

Quito, at around 9700 feet above sea level, boasts an eternal spring climate. At that elevation, however, solar radiation makes exposure to the sun feel extremely warm, while shade temperatures are uncomfortably cold. The upper slopes of the Andes, fringing the settled areas, are called *paramos*. These are the humid tall grasslands signifying wasteland. Although the temperatures are too cool for trees to grow, the *paramos* serve as pasturage for sheep.

The eastern zone of Ecuador encompasses a vast, essentially un-inhabited area which adds up to an economic zero as far as contributing much to that nation's economy. It may be that a north-south marginal highway east of the Andes will help to stimulate development in this wilderness.

As with Peru and Bolivia, Ecuador has a large Indian population in the highlands, grading into a more mestizo population in the Guayas low-lands. The highest proportions of people with Spanish ancestors are found in cities.

The Andean area produces goods for local consumption; it is also the predominant zone of livestock raising (beef cattle and sheep) within the country. The east is largely unexploited except for the extraction of forest products such as balsa wood, rubber, tannin, and hard cabinet woods. Subsistence crops such as maize, beans, potatoes, fruits and vegetables, in addition to the commercial plantation crops of cacao, coffee, and bananas, are grown on the Guayas lowlands. Mineral exploitation has been small compared to Ecuador's neighboring Andean countries, although there are some oil fields west of Guayaquil.

The significance of the Andes mountains in a country like Ecuador is different from their significance in a relatively prosperous country such as Venezuela whose gross productivity is sufficient to generate tax reve-nues for building roads, railroads, and other communication systems. Ecuador has a small population of low productivity. There are some iso-lated basins where the life of the eighteenth century can still be observed almost unchanged.

Ecuador can be summed up as comprising a traditional and a modern aspect. The traditional aspect is focused on the highlands, and the capital city of Quito reflects this tradition. It is the center of government and, until a few years ago, was the primate city of the country. However, the limited economic opportunities of the highlands made it possible for Guayaquil, enjoying a recent prosperity, to surge ahead. Today Guaya-quil, with its direct connections by sea and air to the rest of the world, has more people than Quito. It has become a rapidly growing industrial base financed largely through commercial agriculture on the cacao and banana plantations. And so the rivalry between lowland Guayaquil and Andean Quito continues. In the meantime a sizable proportion of the total population, namely the Indians living on a subsistence level, remains outside of the national life.

The Challenge of Diversity in Colombia

Colombia is the only country of South America which boasts a coast-line on two major water bodies, the Pacific Ocean and the Caribbean Sea. Colombia further illustrates a microcosm of the problems of Latin America, mainly the struggle to establish order and coherence out of diversity.

There are three Andean mountain ranges in Colombia—the Cordil-lera Occidental, Cordillera Central, and Cordillera Oriental, within which are located some fourteen major clusters of population. Almost

70 percent of the population is mestizo, 20 percent is of European-Spanish derivation, 7 percent are Indian, and Negroes (mainly of the Choco area) comprise another 5 percent. Indians and mestizo peoples are found mainly in the Andean zones of southern Colombia.

The early civilization of Colombia was the Chibcha tribe whose center was located near present-day Bogotá on the Cordillera Oriental. The Chibchas were sedentary people who had a fairly well developed agriculture in the pre-Conquest period, although they did not match the technical brilliance of the Incas. They were especially proficient, however, in metallurgy, and fabricated gold objects of remarkable beauty.

As in much of Latin America, the early Spanish settlements were founded where gold had been discovered. The gold rush attracted the first settlers and they followed the gold-bearing gravels along the stream beds and eventually the mother lode deposits for over twenty-five years. In the Antioqueño area, the first significant diversifying element on the cultural landscape was the start of coffee plantations after the 1880s. Most of the coffee planters were the descendants of earlier gold miners who stayed on after the mines were depleted. On the well drained middle slopes, around 5000 feet elevation, between the Cauca and Magdalena rivers, coffee was planted in areas of cleared forest. The world market for coffee grew rapidly during the late nineteenth century, and Colombia participated in the general prosperity. In the following decades, the money earned from coffee was invested in local industry so that Medellin, the capital of the Antioquia region, is the leading manufacturing and industrial center within Colombia. Textile mills, using locally produced woolen and cotton yarns, are prominent among the Medellin industries.

Farther south, the Cauca Valley opens up and forms a long narrow flat space in which sugarcane and cattle have provided the economic mainstay of the valley and of the regional capital of Cali. Farther to the west is the remote Chocó area with Quibdo and its thirty-four feet of rainfall per year. This area did attract settlers, certainly not because of its climate, but because of its gold. Negro slaves were brought in many years ago to work the mines, and many of them remained.

The mainly Indian areas of Colombia are limited to higher elevations in the southern part of the country where subsistence farming and grazing are dominant. As one travels southward one is struck by the rather sharp division between mestizo Colombia and Indian Colombia. The cities of Popoyan and Pasto are regional centers within this area of strong indigenous influence.

The eastern *llanos* or savannas of Colombia are used for extensive cattle production. It is a large, sparsely populated country, dominated by three enormous Andean ranges which have to be crossed and recrossed during any east-west or north-south trip across the country. Communications in this area are extremely difficult. The construction of roads is expensive and maintenance costly. During the rainy season it is common for sustained rains to cause landslides and wash out major highways; this means a delay of several days to restore the road to a trafficable condition.

In the mid-twentieth century there has been a peculiar problem which has further hampered Colombia's development: *La Violencia.*

This is a phenomenon which is not well understood and yet accounts for the loss of over half a million Colombian lives since 1941. *La Violencia* is the phenomenon of murder by roving groups of bandits—murder of the population of isolated hamlets for political reasons or murder for no apparent reason.

Despite massive applications of foreign aid and technical assistance, Colombia has had difficulty in maintaining stability and also moving ahead. It is a country of areas which exhibit great diversity in geography, ethnic grouping, class, and economic systems. In the face of such diversity, it is little wonder that the struggle to establish order has been so difficult.

Problems of Oil-Rich Venezuela

Venezuela is the most prosperous country in Latin America by several measures. It is the successor to the place which Argentina enjoyed during the late nineteenth century when Argentina was leading the rest of Latin America in terms of foreign exchange earnings and general prosperity. Today Venezuela has the highest per capita gross national product in Latin America (around $850 per capita in 1970). This is three times the per capita average income for all Latin America.

The physical lineaments of Venezuela are slightly less complex than those of Colombia. A principal point to note, however, is that population is concentrated within fewer areas than in Colombia. The main relief feature is the Andes Cordillera which continues northeastward from the Cordillera Oriental of Colombia, and extends eastward across northern Venezuela.

The main physical divisions of Venezuela are: (*1*) the central highlands, in which Caracas is located, and whose western portion is called by the local name of Cordillera de Merida; (*2*) the Maracaibo Lowlands, where oil was first produced in 1918; (*3*) the Orinoco Llanos, which were famous for their cattle raising as early as 1800 when Alexander von Humboldt traveled through the area, and is outstanding today for the industrial pioneering effort being realized in that area; and (*4*) the Guiana Highlands, a remote, virtual population desert of no economic value at present.

Most of the population of Venezuela is located in and near the central Highlands. The composition is about 66 percent mestizo, 20 percent European, and the rest Indian, Negro, and mulatto. The mulatto and Negro people are mostly concentrated close to the Caribbean coast, the site of Spanish plantations, and the indigenous people are found mainly in the remote Guiana highlands. The Cordillera de Merida, which was closest to the Colombian area of Chibcha influence and was an area whose Indian population was fairly dense in the pre-Conquest period, is largely mestizo.

The outstanding economic fact of life of Venezuela has been the presence and efficient exploitation of petroleum deposits. Over fifty years of petroleum extraction has provided the country with mounting reserves of foreign exchange. With these revenues, the government has been able to develop an excellent paved highway system, build schools, and provide many of the social services which most other Latin American countries are simply too poor to afford. What the data on average per capita income do not show, however, is that the distribution of wealth is extremely uneven. Most of the income from the petroleum sector of the economy touches the lives of very few people. Only several tens of thousands out of ten million Venezuelans are actually employed in the oil industry. It is hard to imagine that the poor subsistence farmer living in the backlands of the Cordillera de Merida benefits much from the oil revenues. In fact, it could be argued that the oil has had an opposite effect. Inflation has made the prices of most everyday commodities, especially food, much higher than they are in the United States. The cost of living in Caracas is notoriously high among the large cities of the world. Under these circumstances Venezuela has been able to buy most of its food supplies abroad at lower prices than they would cost if bought within Venezuela. (There was a time in the 1950s when ice cream and frozen peas used to be flown to Caracas from Miami, Florida!)

In the 1960s, however, there has been a strong effort to diversify the economy of Venezuela by developing more industries within the country, so that the heavy dependence upon petroleum revenues would be minimized, and Venezuela would be prepared for the time when its petroleum deposits eventually run out.

The most striking recent innovation on the Venezuelan landscape is the pioneering industrial venture of the Orinoco basin. This is a multi-phased project centered in Santo Thomé de Guayana, the location of a modern iron and steel mill which has begun operation, and of the enormous Guri Dam, which will provide abundant hydroelectric power to the new industries of this area. The planners have envisaged a great industrial "Ruhr" of Venezuela.

The Orinoco region is blessed not only by the presence of vast iron ore deposits at El Paso and Cerro Bolivar but also by petroleum and, when the Guri Dam is completed, hydroelectric power. It is also accessible to navigable water because the channel of the Orinoco River is dredged regularly by one of the largest dredges afloat. This part of Venezuela is unique within Latin America. Many people recognize the fact that industrial development within Latin America is progressing rapidly, but that practically all of it is located around the capital cities. Furthermore, most people recognize that there are important pioneer areas being opened up by new settlers, yet these are invariably in remote places and are always of an agrarian nature. The unique and most interesting aspect of the Orinoco development is that it is a pioneer undertaking of an industrial nature located several hundred miles from the capital city, far from the zone of concentrated settlement. It is an ambitious project that only a country with the resources of Venezuela could attempt to realize; it remains to be seen whether the plan will succeed. This development represents, of course, still another way of diversifying the economy of Venezuela and of enlarging the opportunities for economic expansion and efficient utilization of the country's resources.

CHAPTER 9
the la plata countries and chile

The Major Regions of Argentina

We have just looked at some of the causes and consequences of Venezuela's becoming the richest country of Latin America in the mid-twentieth century. Although Venezuela's wealth is based on petroleum, Argentina's relative affluence has been due largely to British capital investments in the nineteenth and twentieth centuries.

One of the striking characteristics of Argentina in contrast to many Latin American countries, is that it boasts not only a dominant and primate city (Buenos Aires) which most countries have, but, uniquely, it boasts a dominant economic region, the Humid Pampa. To the person who has traveled from the United States through Mexico, Central America, and South America, finally arriving at the Humid Pampa and Buenos Aires, the overall impression is that he has reached a "European" country. We shall try to describe and interpret some of the reasons why Argentina has become this most non-Latin country of Latin America.

There are four major physical divisions in Argentina: (1) the Andes; (2) the northern region, including the Chaco and the Paraná Plateau; (3) the pampas; and (4) Patagonia. Argentina's Andean region provides another example of the changing morphology of the Andes which one can observe from one end of the continent to the other. In Argentina, the Andes form an extremely dry area to the north where the slopes are barren and where the dominant agents of weathering and erosion (gullying, deflation by the wind, freezing and thawing) are mechanical. In contrast to the aridity of the northern Andes is the glaciated and more humid climate of the southern Andes. It is, in fact, the ice-sculptured aspect of the southern Andes which provides much of the tourist attraction of the National Park of Bariloche and Lake Nahuel Huapi.

The *North of Argentina* includes (1) the Chaco, a tropical scrub forest, with its alternate wet and dry seasons and the widest range of annual average temperatures within South America; (2) Argentina Mesopotamia, called the Entre Rios, literally, "between the rivers"; and (3) the Paraná Plateau area of Missiones Province.

The pampas include not only the humid area radiating three hundred miles from Buenos Aires, but also the Dry Pampa to the west, whose vegetation is a scrub *monte* type exhibiting distinctly xerophytic characteristics. *Patagonia* is the dry windy plateau in southern Argentina which experiences the passage of Antarctic air masses and the high winds associated with squalls. Its basic aridity, however, stems mainly from its location within the rainshadow of the Andes, and the dominant west-to-east movement of air in those latitudes.

The movement of people throughout Argentina's history has resulted in two main zones of settlement. The first is the piedmont area of the Andes in northwestern Argentina where colonial towns were established with political and economic links to the mining towns of Peru and Bolivia. It was this piedmont zone that became the mule-breeding ground and the supply center for the mining zones of the altiplano. (Mules could not be bred at the higher elevations of the altiplano.) A second zone of settlement was the Humid Pampa, which developed only during the last hundred years. Most casual observers of Argentina are unaware of the distinct geographical division between the Andean piedmont of the colonial period and the Humid Pampa, which is a very recent historical phenomenon.

Buenos Aires is the largest city of the entire Southern Hemisphere. It is the second largest Latin city in the world, after Paris. The degree to which the Humid Pampa has concentrated the life of the country within a small area is evidenced by the fact that the Humid Pampa encompasses only 22 percent of the area of Argentina, and yet it has two-thirds of the nation's population. The Humid Pampa has 70 percent of the railroads, 85 percent of the automobiles, 86 percent of the production of cereals and flax, and 63 percent of the cattle. In other words, the Humid Pampa contributes four-fifths of the total productivity of all Argentina. One advantage of this phenomenon is obvious: namely, that problems of communication are minimized when such a large proportion of the country's population and productive capacity is concentrated within a small area of great fertility and easy access.

Another impressive characteristic of Argentina is the massive European immigration which radically transformed the country over the last century. In 1930 as many as three-fourths of the Argentines were born of European parents, and one-fourth of the population were themselves immigrants. In the 1960s approximately 97 percent of the Argentine population was of European ancestry; only 3 percent of the population were Indian, located in remote areas of the south and west; there were virtually no Negroes.

Argentina was originally settled by people from Peru, Paraguay, and

Chile. The earliest attempt to establish Buenos Aires in 1536 failed because of the warlike Indians who drove off the Spaniards. A permanent settlement was finally established in 1580 but only after Asunción had been founded in 1537. Buenos Aires was but a toehold on the eastern seaboard. Northwestern Argentina, on the other hand, was successfully settled from Lima, Peru, over the Andes, between 1551 and 1592. The original indigenous inhabitants were crowded out of those areas of European influence and were gradually pushed southward across the pampas. The Indians and the mestizos (gaucho) learned to use horses (as did the Great Plains Indians of the early United States) and sometimes made life uncomfortable for the Spaniards by raiding their outpost communications and stealing cattle. The Indians were clever entrepreneurs: they drove their stolen cattle across the Andes and sold them to the Chileans. There were many instances of Indian-Spanish hostilities before the nineteenth century when it was decided to eliminate the Indian threat. This policy, carried out by General Rocas, succeeded in exterminating most of the pampa Indians and driving the rest to remote reserves to the south and west.

MAN'S TRANSFORMATION OF THE PAMPAS AND THE ESTANCERO'S WORLD. Argentina has been largely an invention by Europeans in contrast to such countries as Peru, Bolivia, or Ecuador which reflect not only the transplanted sixteenth century Spanish culture, but also strong indigenous influences which pervade many aspects of contemporary culture. Argentina exhibits, probably better than any other country within Latin America, a high degree of Europeanization of the landscape.

Oscar Schmeider, a German geographer, has done research in the La Plata area tracing the evolution of the Argentine Pampa through all the various stages of its development.[1] Schmeider argues that the lush verdant grasslands of the Pampas, which were so widely praised and publicized in Western Europe and the United States during the nineteenth century, represented only the most recent phase of a long period of adjustment and adaptation which began long before the arrival of Europeans in the New World. Schmeider cites the journals of early Spanish travelers through the Pampa who mentioned the presence of large areas of trees and *monte* vegetation (drought-resistant broad leaf forest, twenty to thirty feet tall), that was considerably denser than it is today. He further states that the *monte* vegetation of the Pampa had already been considerably reduced by Indian burnings for the purpose of hunting and warfare. This decimated vegetation was what the Spanish explorers observed in the early sixteenth century when they tried to establish permanent communities in Argentina.

The next phase was the conversion of the coarse, tough pasture grasses (*pasto duro*) into the succulent *pasto tierno* on which horses and cattle brought by the Spaniards to Argentina could graze. Cattle and

[1] Oscar Schmeider, "The Pampa—A Natural or Culturally Induced Grassland?" University of California Publications in Geography, Vol. 2, No. 8 (September 1927), 255–70.

horses literally transformed the surface of the earth by trampling it with their hooves and by breaking the sod, which had never been cut by a plow. The introduction of European pasture grasses and the addition of the animal manure transformed the coarse-grassed pastures into the ideal grazing areas for which Argentina has become justly famous.

Before 1853 the Pampa was the *estancero*'s world, in which the dominant figure was the man on horseback. In this cattle culture, there was no place for farming and agriculture. The law of that era fully supported the cattle-raising point of view, discouraging early initiatives in agriculture. It was a form of monoculture based upon the raising of livestock. The entire range was open. The absence of fences meant that travel between two points just followed a straight line, with no need to turn off to one side or the other. The very flatness of the Pampa made it possible to haul large wagons with enormous wheels by oxen right across the Pampa surface. There was no compulsion to build true roads.

In the northwestern part of Argentina, the colonial settlement was firmly established, and its economy was based upon mule trading with the Andean countries of Peru and Bolivia, as previously mentioned. Two of the outstanding piedmont towns were Tucuman, which has since evolved into an important sugar producing area, and Mendoza, now famous for its vineyards. Mesopotamia was peripheral to the early colonial penetrations of the northwest, and too far afield to experience any influence from Buenos Aires. It remained a flat, inaccessible place where the presence of large rivers posed a formidable barrier. The Chaco was good only for the extraction of *quebracho* wood from which tannin could be extracted. Patagonia remained an unexploited area until European settlement there after the 1870s. Its cool dry climate and low population density made it a center of sheep raising, and only in the protected river oases, such as those of the Rio Negro and Rio Colorado, have fruit orchards thrived.

The Humid Pampa has a continuum of humidity conditions, ranging from moist on the east to dry on the west. The dependability of rainfall decreases as one moves from east to west. It was in and around Buenos Aires that the core of European settlement occurred on the eastern seaboard of southern South America. The scope and range of European impact did not extend more than about 100 miles out from Buenos Aires as recently as 100 years ago. A system of forts was constructed along a so-called *frontera* or fortified zone, which separated the Hispanic area surrounding Buenos Aires from the untamed hinterland where the security of life and property could not be so easily guaranteed. The positioning of the *frontera* followed more or less the line of the Rio Salado for many acres. It was within this protected area that the cattle culture and the *estancero*'s world prevailed.

THE ARRIVAL OF FARMERS AND MODERNIZATION OF THE HUMID PAMPA. Before 1853, the Humid Pampa of Argentina was cattle country. The change from cattle ranching to farming brought about a radical transformation of the landscape. What happened after 1850 was the introduction of agriculture in an area where the prevailing economic and social system allowed no place for farmers or for crops.

Developments in Argentina's Humid Pampa followed similar developments in the Great Plains of the United States by about twenty-five to thirty years. Both areas had been dominated by cattle ranching. The devices which allowed farmers to domesticate the plains have been documented by Walter Prescott-Webb in his engrossing book *The Great Plains.* They included the invention of barbed wire, the windmill for drawing up deeply located water supplies, the invention of the steel plow which enabled the man with his horse-drawn plow to cut for the first time the thick sod, and finally the Colt six-shot repeating pistol which enabled the frontiersman-farmer to defend himself. The advance of a frontier of settlement across prime agricultural land in both the Great Plains and the Humid Pampa occurred at a time when markets for those agricultural commodities were expanding in Europe and in the United States. Also important was a system of credits which allowed the financing of many agricultural ventures.

The expanding markets for beef in Europe became available to Argentina because of the invention of the refrigerated ship which allowed chilled beef carcasses to be shipped all the way from Argentina to Europe. Because the *estanceros* were unable to provide the manpower required to prepare pasturelands for their stock, they encouraged immigration of tenant farmers from Europe. These immigrants cleared the *monte*, planted food crops for their own use, and then left that cleared land planted in alfalfa which could yield up to three cuttings per year for the *estancero's* cattle. The *estancero* encouraged tenant agriculture only as a means of preparing the *monte* land for relatively intensive livestock grazing. The growing market for wheat complicated the picture, and made it tempting to invest in wheat production. In the decades following 1850 there developed an increasing degree of interdependence between the farmers and the *estanceros.* One of the earliest agricultural colonies was Santa Fé, which survived because of a remote location where it was free to innovate with commercial grain growing and to reach new technical and marketing solutions in terms of establishing working relations between men and the land. Very soon after these early successes in agriculture, as at Santa Fé, came the extension of railroad lines across the Humid Pampa. In 1857 the first railroad was laid out into the hinterland from Buenos Aires. The previous roads were nothing more than ruts across the landscape. There were no fences, and trails ran in all directions. Most railroads were built between 1857 and 1910 and were financed not by the *estanceros,* who had their capital tied up in land and livestock, but by British capital. The rolling stock was British, and the trains were fueled by British coal. At a breathtaking rate, the railway lines were laid out under the most ideal conditions, and booming land values accompanied them. In the last analysis, it was the lack of population before 1850 which contributed to the underdeveloped status of the Humid Pampa. People were needed to populate the Pampa and to valorize it. Beginning in 1856 the German, French, and Swiss immigrants, and in succeeding decades, many millions of people sought a new life in Argentina. Some of the labor was seasonal; there were many immigrants who returned to their homelands periodically. They were called *golondrinos* (or swallows) because they followed the farm work seasons between Europe and Argentina.

We have seen how the confrontation between the different technologies, namely livestock raising and commercial agriculture, became resolved within the Humid Pampa. The cleavage between a society built essentially upon livestock raising and that based upon agriculture continues to cut across Argentine society so that even today, one can talk in terms of the social and political aspects of these two distinctly different ways of life.

Since World War II, Argentina has had many problems trying to maintain its productivity in the face of rising costs of government and the provision of numerous social services at a time when the productivity of labor has not increased at a comparable rate. Inflation has also discouraged certain kinds of investment in Argentina. In this sense, Argentina has shared some of the problems of its neighbor Uruguay, across the La Plata estuary. It is ironic that this country which made such spectacular and innovative gains in truly modernizing agriculture in the late nineteenth century has failed to maintain this early advantage in the middle of the twentieth century. Some observers wonder why Argentina, with more advantages than most Latin American countries, has not progressed further than it has, and they see some justification in the political difficulties which the country has experienced in recent decades.

Problems of Landlocked Paraguay

The history of Paraguay has been intimately entwined with that of its neighbors, Argentina, Uruguay, and Brazil. Paraguay appears to have been left with the fewest advantages of all the La Plata lands. Argentina is blessed with a large national territory, vast areas of fertile land, and free access to navigable water. Uruguay has the fertility and access to water but lacks the great size and diversified ecology of Argentina. Paraguay, on the other hand, is not only small, but also lacks sizable areas of important resources. Tucked away in the remote center of the South American continent, Paraguay has been largely bypassed by the modernizing currents of the twentieth century. It is rather like an eddy away from the main streams of development.

Paraguay can be divided into two main regions. Western Paraguay belongs to the greater region of the Chaco, that vast monotonous lowland of alternately wet and dry conditions which has little in the way of resources or population, and which has not added much to the economic life of the country as a whole. In Eastern Paraguay, that area between the Paraguay and Paraná rivers, most of the population and most of the productive land is found. Rainfall is higher here, up to 80 inches per year, and the higher fertility of soils in some areas can be traced to the presence of weathered diabase lava formations.

The colonial period witnessed important missionary activities which could flourish in such a remote area. Jesuit missionaries established several centers where runaway Indians and slaves gathered, fleeing the onerous work burdens and living conditions imposed by their Spanish and Portuguese masters. The Jesuit missions became so strong that pressure was brought to bear upon the mother countries by the property-owning masters to expel them; this was finally accomplished in 1767.

Asunción was one of the earliest capital cities of the New World, being founded in 1537. At that time, only Lima, Peru, and Potosï, in Bolivia, were larger. In the sixteenth century Asunción was indeed one of the more exciting places in which to live. There were no outstanding gold, silver, or diamond discoveries in Paraguay to draw settlers as occurred in sixteenth-century Mexico and Peru, or even in eighteenth-century Brazil. And in the era of independence from Spain, Paraguay has suffered from a lack of contact with the outside world.

There is probably no other country in all of Latin America where the fate of an individual state has been more closely linked to the influence of a handful of individual persons. A series of strong dictators ruled the country in the decades following independence, most notable of whom were Dr. Francia (ruled 1811–40), Carlos Lopez, and his son Francisco Solano Lopez. Francisco Lopez precipitated the incredible Paraguayan War (1865–70) in which Paraguay fought against Uruguay, Argentina, and Brazil. At the war's outset, Paraguay boasted the largest standing army within all of South America.

The adult male population was largely decimated during that war. It took many decades for Paraguay to recover its earlier population status. Again, in 1933, a war with Bolivia, over the Chaco, took a heavy toll of life and property. It has been only since World War II that stronger links with the outside world have been actively pursued. For example, Asunción connects with the Atlantic Ocean by way of a highway. The port of Paranaguá, in the state of Paraná in southern Brazil, is linked by road with Asunción, and is envisaged as a free port for Paraguay. There is, however, not much cargo which moves over that particular route all the way from Paranaguá to Asunción.

Well over half of Paraguay's population is engaged in farming or forestry, and most of the agriculture is of a subsistence nature. The main crops are maize and manioc. Rice has shown a gain in recent years and sugarcane and fruit production have also risen in response to government encouragement and incentives. Most of the good farmland, however, is owned by a small number of landlords. The majority of farmers own little or no land.

The main link with the world outside is, of course, the Paraguay River, with only a skeleton network of roads radiating outward from Asunción. It is a small country with a small population, but unlike other small countries such as Israel, Belgium, or even Uruguay, Paraguay has, unfortunately, a small productive capacity and few prospects of improving this rather solemn picture.

Uruguay: A Welfare State Built Upon a Pastoral Base

Uruguay emerges in striking contrast to Paraguay, although both are about the same size. Why has the development of Uruguay been so different? Has it been due to natural or physical conditions, or to the kinds of people who settled there?

In physical terms, Uruguay strongly resembles the Humid Pampa of Argentina, except there is slightly more rolling terrain and hilly land in Uruguay than in the Humid Pampa. Almost all of the total national territory of Uruguay is arable; it has been blessed with a natural fertility which has been exploited for several hundred years.

In common with Paraguay, Chile, or Argentina, the people of Uruguay are concentrated in one large nucleus of population. One third of the nation's population of three million is clustered in and around the capital city of Montevideo. None of the other cities of Uruguay begin to approach the population of the primate city: they all have less than 100,000 people. Over 90 percent of the people are of pure European-Spanish descent, with some 8 percent mestizo and 2 percent Negroes. There are practically no Indians. Uruguay, in the eyes of many observers, is a very effective buffer state between the two giants of South America, Argentina and Brazil. In its early history, Uruguay was actually occupied at one time or another by Argentina and by Brazil, but since its formation into a sovereign state, it has played the role of a buffer state very effectively.

The early occupance and land use of Uruguay are similar to that of the Humid Pampa: namely the conversion of the tough native grasses to a more suitable grazing forage through the introduction of improved European pasture grasses. Not only beef cattle but also sheep have thrived on these pastures. In fact, the original fertility of the soil might be now viewed as something of a disadvantage since the *estanceros* never thought of applying fertilizer in those early decades. The land was so rich that it continued to yield pasture grasses year after year, and there was little or no thought given to fertilizing or fallowing land in order to maintain its productive capacity.

Cattle were brought into Uruguay by 1603 through Argentine cattle buyers. The middle nineteenth century witnessed the infusion of British capital. In 1840 high quality Merino sheep were introduced, and in 1864 the Fray Bentos meat packing plant was built. In 1868 the first railroad was constructed. In the 1870s barbed wire was introduced, and refrigerated ships began to carry beef carcasses to Europe.

Within the last twenty years, the productivity of Uruguay's land and economy has not risen proportionately with the costs of supporting Uruguayan society. Uruguay has not experienced the violent upheavals or suffered the depredations of self-seeking dictators that some other countries have suffered. It has been peaceful and prosperous for many decades, and for these reasons, has been called the Switzerland of South America. At the same time, this democratic and enlightened government instituted social reforms and welfare programs financed by its earnings from overseas exports. Some of this legislation was far ahead of its time. It is possible for some Uruguayans to retire at the age of fifty. There are many government services which have been provided and which, of course, have cost large amounts of money.

Now, however, the funds from which these welfare programs were financed have diminished. Some Uruguayans have recognized that the fault lies in the failure of the livestock and agricultural sectors of the economy, that is, the dominant sector, to hold onto its leading position by modernizing production techniques. In other words, profits have not been plowed back into maintaining the productivity of the land which is the productive base of the entire national economy. The result, which can be seen as one travels throughout Uruguay today, is the extensive overgrazing and serious incipient erosion of the sloping land. The pastures have not been regenerated, the soils have not been renewed, and the meat or agricultural yields per hectare of crops have declined.

A series of devaluations of the Uruguayan peso and the spiraling inflation of the post-World War II decades have made life for the average Uruguayan very difficult. It is hard to be optimistic for Uruguay's economy if the productivity of the land is not substantially raised in the near future.

The Three Faces of Chile

The long narrow slope of Chile does not at first glance reveal the rather conventional distribution pattern of population and productivity within the Latin American context. Despite its pencil shape, most of the Chilean people and most of the effective national territory are located in a small area of middle Chile.

The Central Valley of Chile runs north-south and is flanked on the east by the mighty Andes and on the west by the lower coastal range. It is fairly well isolated from Peru to the north, and Argentina to the east except for a few surface and air links. On the other hand, it is the only area within Latin America which has a Mediterranean climate, and this factor provides Chile with certain advantages, such as good vineyards and the ability to produce "winter" crops. The "winter-rain–summer-droughts" characteristic of all Mediterranean-type climates confers special advantage, in that Chile can supply world food markets with fresh fruits and vegetables out of the regular growing season.

There are three distinct parts of the country.

Northern Chile is the dry area of the Atacama Desert. This lies north of the Aconcagua River and the only moisture encountered in some coastal locations is the *garua,* or coastal fog, whereby moisture is applied to the land and plants by condensation and not by precipitation. There is no agricultural reason for the north to be important; it is the accident of geology and climate which has made the Atacama valuable to Chile.

In the Atacama, an upland valley which trends north-south for some 500 miles at an elevation between 3000 and 6000 feet above sea level, lie great beds of sodium nitrate and other valuable salts which have accumulated there from the adjacent mountain slopes over millennia. The great economic value of these deposits has justified the piping-in of water over long distances and the maintenance of an industrial labor force in this inhospitable area.

Before World War II, Chilean nitrates were widely sought by world markets for fertilizer and for the making of gunpowder. In recent decades, however, the market for Chilean nitrate fertilizers has declined because of technological innovations whereby nitrogen can be extracted directly from the atmosphere. As a result, the importance of this mainstay of the earlier years has diminished.

Middle Chile, the prime agricultural region of the country, lies between the Acongagua River to the north and the Bio-Bio River south of Concepción. In this narrow valley lie fertile alluvial and volcanic soils, watered by perennial streams which flow from the melting snows on the Andes to the east despite the summer dry season. Irrigation by sprinklers permits the growing of subtropical fruits in this area. Despite the great suitability of the Central Valley for agriculture, a large proportion of it remains devoted to extensive grazing. This is due to the traditional dominance of the large land holding, the *hacienda,* and the fact that land taxes have always been low enough to permit less efficient and less productive kinds of land utilization to prevail.

The southern part of Middle Chile is an area of farms and forests which is outstanding because of the important nineteenth- and twentieth-century European colonization of that area. The original Spanish settlers and their descendents remained mainly in the central valley of northern Middle Chile, leaving the densely forested lands of southernmost Middle Chile untouched. In fact, those are the areas, extending as far south as Chiloe Island, to which the warlike Araucanian Indians were eventually banished. It is interesting to observe how the German colonists were able to valorize the area and make it productive by bringing different attitudes and techniques of land use to the forested areas.

Southern Chile still remains a formidable area, with its spectacular glaciated landscapes of rugged mountains, glaciers, dense forests, a climate with up to 100 inches of rain per year, and considerable amounts of snow in the higher areas during winter. This wet, tempestuous part of Chile extends southward all the way to Tierra Del Fuego where the only inhabitants are a few sheep raisers and the remnants of marginal Indian tribes. Southern Chile can be considered as an area essentially outside the effective national territory, in contrast to Middle Chile and some of northern Chile.

Chile enjoyed relative prosperity from the export of nitrate during the nineteenth century, and it is fortunate in having been able to diversify into other mining ventures (copper, iron ore) and industrial development in this century. There are, however, many social problems which remain unresolved. Although Chile has a growing middle class, efforts at liberal government have not been able to effectively redistribute resources and wealth in the country, nor yet realize the hopes for basic social reforms.

The world watches to see whether the socialist government of President Allende, elected in 1970, can solve Chile's problems.

Chile's agriculture benefits from the great variety of ecologies which extend from low latitude to higher, middle latitude regions. There is a considerable amount of crop diversification within cultivated areas. A basic problem, however, is the small market available to Chile. Its distance from major world markets is greater than that from any other Latin American country. Despite the serious problems Chile has faced, its chances for success will be improved if, in a climate of political stability, the basic economic and social reforms which have been begun, can be carried out.

The Land and People of Brazil

Brazil takes up about half the area of South America, and contributes half of its population. In an area slightly larger than the continental United States, Brazil contains approximately 100 million people as of 1971. Its immense size poses unique problems and questions. The country is so vast and encompasses such a wide variety of human experiences at the present time that it seems a microcosm of the physical and historical world. In human terms, Brazil can be regarded as a laboratory of racial assimilation and cultural mixture. It is an area which has stood out among other Latin American countries as having had the fewest political revolutions, and those that did occur were largely bloodless.

The physical geography of Brazil is extremely diversified. The land can be divided into two categories: (*1*) the lowlands, largely of tertiary deposits in the Amazon, and (*2*) the highlands, which in no way compare to the Andes in elevation, but have distinct characteristics which profoundly affect life and livelihood in those areas. About half of the highlands area is less than 650 feet above sea level with only 4 percent being over 3000 feet. Twelve peaks rise over 7000 feet.

The principal rivers of Brazil drain toward the center of the country, not toward the coast. As mentioned in the introductory chapter, the most populated areas, the south and east, are not commercially served by the rivers, since their direction, orientation, and manner of flow make them mostly unnavigable.

Underlying the land surfaces of the country, and outcropping in some significant places in eastern Brazil are the crystalline basement rocks, which weather to fairly fertile agricultural soils where the sedimentary cover has been removed by geological weathering.

Brazilian snow scene, ten miles north of Santa Maria, Rio Grande do Sul, in August 1965. The southern plateau of Brazil receives snow every winter, but it lasts only a few days.

Brazil has many climates. Most famous, of course, are the humid-tropical conditions in the Amazon Basin. Few people realize that it snows regularly in southern Brazil during the winter, and that there is an enormous area of true desert in the interior of Northeast Brazil. The highest temperatures, surprisingly, are not found in the Amazon North, where at Santarem the absolute maximum and minimum temperatures are 93°F and 65°F respectively; much higher temperatures are found at low elevations in Northeast Brazil. Here 106°F have been observed in places of low humidity where the insolation (or sun's radiant energy) at the earth's surface has great intensity and where night temperatures fall sharply from rapid radiation of heat back to space.

The latitudinal fluctuation of the Intertropical Convergence Zone (a zone of warm tropical air moving toward low latitudes from the subtropics, causing uplift and heavy precipitation) is the mechanism which brings the summer season of rains to most of northern and central Brazil. Southern Brazil, on the other hand, enjoys a moderate rainfall which is distributed fairly evenly throughout the year. The peculiarities of the rainfall distribution in Northeast Brazil mean that in certain years, depending upon the size and strength of a monsoon-like indraft of maritime tropical air off the Atlantic Ocean, the interior areas may not receive rain. These periodic droughts are part of the physical and historical fabric in Northeast Brazil.

The basic vegetation types in Brazil are forest, savanna, grasslands, tropical thorn forest (*caatinga*) and softwood (*araucaria*) forests. The equatorial forests (*mata equatorial*) of the Amazon Basin cover less than half of the nation's total area. This is the region of the *lianas* and *epiphytes,* sustained by temperatures in the seventies and eighties and high relative humidities. It is also an area of low soil fertility. The shallow-rooted crops, like maize and manioc, which have been planted where the forest has been cleared by slash-and-burn methods, give decreasing yields as that small layer of partially decomposed forest litter is exhausted.

A second variety of *mata,* the semideciduous evergreen forests of eastern Brazil, comprise areas of fertile land and are eagerly sought out by farmers. The very word *mata* is synonymous with fertile farmland. These areas of *mata* are sharply distinguished from those of the savanna (*campo cerrado*), the grasslands covered by scattered trees that are famous for their sterility. The savannas are mainly used as grazing lands for extensive-type cattle raising or as places from which to gather firewood for charcoal.

The thorn scrub forest (or *caatinga*) of Northeast Brazil is a truly xerophytic vegetation. Part of the drought-resistant characteristic of plants there is from the dry climate, but part is also from the "desertification" of the land by repeated clearing, burning, and cropping cycles which provide an increasingly infertile setting for plants.

In southern Brazil, in the state of Paraná, grow the softwood forests of the *araucaria* tree or, popularly termed, "Paraná pine." These are of a geologically ancient variety which has somehow survived from the Paleozoic era. The *araucaria* forests form the basis for a fairly large lumber industry. The high rate at which the trees are being felled in Santa Catarina and Paraná means that the *araucaria* trees will disappear by 2000 A.D. unless extensive reforestation is carried out.

POPULATION.   The people of Brazil cover a broad spectrum beginning with the indigenous peoples who spoke languages of the Tupi-Guaraní family and who numbered possibly as many as one million when the Portuguese landed in 1500. The pre-Conquest Indians were essentially hunters and gatherers and subsistence farmers. None of these tribes, however, had developed the social, political or technological attainments of the Aztecs, Mayas or Incas.

The Portuguese arrived in Brazil in 1500 when Pedro Alvarez Cabral landed in southern Bahia. They were themselves a mixture of Celtic and Nordic peoples with strains of Mediterranean, Moorish, and Semitic origins. Northern Portugal was inhabited by peoples whose original Swabian roots went back to Central Europe, so that to view the Portuguese settlers as a single type or kind is clearly a mistake.

Brazil's third major population element is the African. Negro slaves were brought over in the 1530s to work on the sugarcane plantations, and this influx continued until slavery was abolished there in 1888.

In addition to these three principal groups, there were later immigrants, mostly Europeans, who came in the nineteenth century. The most recent immigrants to Brazil are the Japanese who settled in São Paulo and in a few areas of the Amazon North.

BRAZIL'S SETTLEMENT AND THE SUCCESSION OF ECONOMIC BOOMS AND BUSTS.   Much of Brazil's history and geography of settlement can be viewed in terms of the quest for forested (that is to say, fertile) lands. However, the initial discovery and exploration of Brazil derives from quite different motives. In the early colonial period Brazil was inhabited by adventurers who came, not in search of land, but rather to find gold and Indian slaves who could be put to work mining gold. Brazil presented a rather false front to these early explorers. Often they assumed that the whole country was covered with the lush tropical forest that in actuality was a narrow border along the streams they traveled, or that the dissected edge of plateaus in the distance was the foot of a *serra* or mountain range. This, added to the fact that Pedro Alvarez Cabral discovered Brazil by mistake at a time when Portugal was engaged in a thriving and demanding commercial trade with the East Indies, diminished Portugal's interest in the New World. Very simply, Brazil offered few commodities and trade items that Portugal could use.

Some attempts to exploit Brazil's resources were made. One such experiment, the donatory system, failed (see Chapter 1). Nevertheless, a few key cities were successfully established in a short time: Salvador (Bahia) in 1502; São Vicente (in the state of São Paulo) in 1532; Olinda (Pernambuco) in 1537; São Paulo in 1554; and Rio de Janeiro in 1567. Still it must be stressed that Portugal's interest in colonies was essentially economic, and Brazil, which appeared to offer little in the way of wealth, was not considered as a matter of first importance.

Perhaps as a result of this first impression, Brazil's economic history is distinctly cyclical: a series of economic booms followed by equally spectacular declines. Many observers feel that throughout history the Brazilians have been much too interested in fast speculative gain, too impatient for the slow, steady nurturing of the nation's resources and productive capacities that would produce long-term yield to the entrepreneurs, their descendents, and to the country in general. Many, in fact, feel that this cyclical history is a major defect in Brazil's development.

The first economic cycle, which only lasted from 1500 to 1550, was based on brazilwood and involved the establishment of *feitorias* (factories) where the brazilwood (a dyewood) was brought in, collected, and then shipped out to Europe. This activity took place in the tropical forests of northern and Northeastern Brazil, and never gave rise to any significant permanent settlement. For that time, the great importance and commercial significance of dyes such as brazilwood (red), indigo (blue), and cochineal (red) cannot be overestimated. Such dyes were the main sources for coloring fabrics, cosmetic products, and paints and inks in the sixteenth century.

The second cycle was the sugarcane cycle, beginning around 1532 with the introduction of sugarcane from the Portuguese Madeira Islands off the coast of northwest Africa. African slaves brought shortly afterwards provided the manpower whereby cultivation developed rapidly to fill the growing demands in Europe. A steady rise in production in the humid coastal *zona da mata* of Northeast Brazil, from Salvador to Natal, reached its peak between 1650 and 1700. Thereafter there was a relative decline. Sugarcane is still produced today, although on a marginal economic basis.

Gold and diamonds were discovered for the first time (after almost 200 years in Brazil's colonial history) in the interior of Minas Gerais, about 200 miles north of Rio de Janeiro, in the 1690s. The *bandeirantes* (literally, flag-bearers), who had scoured Brazil and tramped over much of South America for almost 150 years in search of gold, finally succeeded. The gold deposits were first found in the gravels of the Rio das Velhas, northeast of present-day Belo Horizonte.

This discovery of mineral wealth was important for two reasons. First, in the Spanish-Portuguese competition for colonies in the New World, Portugal had always been behind. The presence of gold and diamonds obviously made Brazil a more attractive place to explorers, colonists, prospectors, and speculators—just about anyone! Second, the fact that the gold and diamonds of Brazil were located far from the coast (near Ouro Preto and Diamantina, respectively) led to the first significant settlements in the interior. From that time onward, the currents of settlement have been away from the coast and into the center of Brazil. The idea of *interiorização* (interiorization) and the famous *marcha para o oeste* (march to the west) exhortation of former president Getulio Vargas are key themes in Brazil's history.

The next outstanding economic boom was based on coffee, for which the world market demands grew after 1850. The search for new lands in which to plant coffee attracted settlement southward and westward into the states of São Paulo, northern Paraná, and eventually, today, Mato Grosso. Great fortunes were made in coffee and much of the money gravitated toward the financial, banking, and credit center of the city of São Paulo where it has been reinvested to build the industrial complex which has since evolved.

A rubber boom flourished in the Amazon Basin of northern Brazil in the short period between 1880 and 1912. The world market price of natural rubber rose because of the growing demand for rubber tires for automobiles, trucks, buses, and bicycles. As the price of rubber soared, speculators rushed to the Amazon to participate in the prosperity. Competition from plantation-grown rubber of the Malay peninsula burst this speculative bubble, however, and the market price collapsed by 1913.

A contemporary boom since 1945 has focused upon the urban building industries. Apartments have been constructed at a spectacular rate and rapid valorization of urban land has occurred as the influx of people to cities grows. Of course, part of the urban building cycle has been stimulated by Brazil's inflation and the postwar devaluation of the *cruzeiro*. People sought to protect the purchasing power of their *cruzeiros* by investing in real estate or hard goods like automobiles and refrigerators. In the 1960s the raising of beef cattle expanded so rapidly that it might almost be called an economic boom.

While these various economic booms and busts were succeeding one another, a large segment of the Brazilian population continued to exist on subsistence agriculture. The characteristic method of farming in Brazil is a system of land rotation or slash-and-burn farming whereby the farmer clears his plot of land by cutting down the trees and bushes and allowing them to dry throughout the dry season. He burns over the land just before the summer rains and plants his maize, beans, manioc, sometimes some rice and some fruits and vegetables. The average farmer does not apply fertilizer, nor does he engage in any modern methods of contour plowing or even use machinery, but this is the general pattern which characterizes subsistence farming. Subsistence agriculture is thus the background against which other, spectacular developments occur.

The general context, however, of the post-1955 period has been one of general inflation where the industrial sector of Brazil has developed while the agricultural and rural sectors have languished. And it is the devaluation of the *cruzeiro* which has stimulated and paid for much of the new industrial development and even for the building of the new capital, Brasília. It remains to be seen whether Brazil will continue this tradition of economic cycles or whether different patterns of sustained growth will emerge.

Northeast Brazil: The Culture Hearth of the Nation

Many of the formative influences that have shaped Brazil first appeared in the distinctive Northeast of the nation. It was here that Brazilian society was forged and many of the social institutions that have become an integral part of present-day life originated. The basic lineaments of the strongly patriarchal "sugar society," based upon slavery, were established in the early sixteenth century; the dominant modes and systems of land use were also outlined at that time and have changed little in the subsequent centuries. Some writers have compared the role of the Northeast to that of New England in the United States. It is here that the first permanent settlements were established by the Portuguese in the early sixteenth century. Like New England, it is composed of small states that have had a disproportionately strong influence on its nation's history in terms of its contribution of statesmen and distinguished men of arts and letters. Unlike New England, however, the Northeast of Brazil comprises the largest underdeveloped area of the entire Western Hemisphere, and is geographically unique, in that it has the only desert in the country.

The brief dyewood boom in Northeast Brazil (1500–50) was followed by almost 200 years of prosperity derived from sugarcane plantations. Much of our knowledge of this colonial period has come from writers of the Northeast itself. As noted earlier, sugarcane was imported from Madeira, and its cultivation depended heavily on slaves brought from Africa (beginning in 1538). Because land was usually obtained in the form of *sesmarias* or grants, the planter's capital was tied up in slaves. Gilberto Freyre's primary work in social history, *The Masters and the Slaves*, documents the daily life and social significance of the sugarcane plantation, the Negro slave quarters, and the close interdependence of the African slaves and their Portuguese masters. There was much economic gain to be made through sugarcane; plantations dominated the colonial period in Northeast Brazil.

As sugar dominated the coast of the Northeast, beef cattle dominated its interior. The vast wilderness of *caatinga* provided ample area to raise cattle despite the unfavorable physical conditions. The *sertão* (or dry grassland) is not fertile enough for agriculture, but cattle can survive on it. Between the humid coast and the dry *sertão*, there has evolved a kind of symbiotic balance: sugarcane and other fruits and vegetables grown in the west *zona da mata* are exchanged for leather products, beef, and manioc from the *sertão*. Many of these items have been exchanged traditionally at intermediate cities in the transitional zone of the *agreste*.

Each of the three zones has its own distinct ecology, its own economy, and, in many ways, its own society. The cattle culture of the interior for several centuries maintained a strict separation from the *zona da mata*, and the intermediate *agreste* remained a buffer zone and also a zone of exchange between the coast and the interior.

DESERTS, FORESTS, AND THE LEGACY OF THE LAND IN NORTHEAST BRAZIL. The interior of the Northeast has suffered many severe droughts throughout its recorded history. Even old Indian legends tell of them. These droughts occur when the expected fall rainy season does not arrive. Whether or not a particular place receives rains depends upon the strength and size and influence of three different air masses of precipitation. There are dependable winter rains brought by polar air masses moving northward in winter along the coast. There are dependable summer and fall rains to the west, and autumn rains to the northeast. These are tied to the strong low pressure cell which moves into South America and spreads eastward to Northeast Brazil. Whether or not a place receives rain or not depends largely upon its orientation and exposure toward the three centers of action.

For many years it was believed that the great poverty of the Northeast was due to the droughts. Government assistance was directed toward providing more water. In fact the federal government set up the IFOCS (Federal Inspectorate of Works Against the Droughts) as early as 1909. Although this organization constructed dams and reservoirs, true irrigation works never resulted from these efforts on the vast scale needed. A lot of *vazante* agriculture was practiced on the wet lands of the reservoirs as the water slowly evaporated once the rains had filled the reservoir. Before the water level would rise, at the beginning of the next year's rainy season, the farmers would have had time to harvest their subsistence crops. The successor of IFOCS was DNOCS (National Department of Works Against the Droughts), which continued to improve the water supply but also branched out into other related activities.

It was not until the 1950s with the Bank of the Northeast and its successor, SUDENE, that attention was drawn to the man-made causes of poverty, i.e., lack of forage due to overgrazing, lack of financing by banks, lack of marketing systems. Most of the land in the Northeast, of course, is owned by a small percentage of the population. The history of land use in the area is a document of destructive exploitation of the soil and vegetation resources with the result that some degree of desertification has occurred in all areas. In an area of sparse and unreliable rainfall, the vegetation and soil cover are highly susceptible to abuse by man through overcropping and overgrazing without the application of land conservation techniques. The droughts of the Northeast, in effect, are as much man-made as they are natural.

A comparison of Philip von Luetzelburg's study of vegetation density in 1910–20 to recent air photography and field work by this writer [1] reveals that in most areas vegetation is much less dense today than it was early in this century. The rate of deforestation has accelerated because of the cities' increasing demands for charcoal. The extension of paved highways has meant that charcoal buyers are able to reach new charcoal sources deep in the interior of the *caatinga*. Virtually no conservation techniques are practiced in the Northeast. Most farmers plant and cultivate the same way their grandfathers did. The only instance of which I know of contour plowing and strip farming on slopes is the Pesqueira tomato paste factory farm.

It can be said that the legacy of the land is a poor one and that man has chosen *not* to make the most efficient and productive use of the resources at his disposal. A longtime student of Northeast Brazil, José Guimarães Duque, has long argued for the use of more perennial true crops and other xerophytic varieties of plant crops. [2] The usual manner in which farmers treat the dry areas—*as though they were humid*, planting their maize and beans year after year, frequently experiencing failure because of drought—must give way to a new approach to agriculture in this area.

In the 1960s SUDENE invested large amounts of money to bolster the economy of the *sertão*. The attack was mainly on the institutional level through existing government agencies, banks, and educational institutions, and not on the "hydraulic solutions" (i.e., dam building, water storage, etc.) which former government organizations such as IFOCS and DNOCS had emphasized. It is still really too early to evaluate the effectiveness of these efforts.

LAND TENURE, TAXES, AND THE GEOGRAPHY OF POVERTY.   Land taxes in the interior of the Northeast are extremely low: there are large areas where the average land tax is less than a dollar per square mile per year! This means that a farmer is not penalized for inefficiency. He can *afford* to use the land ineffectively or leave it fallow. A discriminatory tax would tend to bring unused land into production, or at least promote its sale by placing a tax burden on unused land. As yet there is no evidence on the results of such legislation. In many instances, such legislation has been passed but not widely enforced.

[1] Kempton E. Webb, *The Changing Face of Northeast Brazil* (Columbia University Press, in press).

[2] José Guimarães Duque, *Solo e Aqua no Poligono das Secas* (D.N.O.C.S., Fortaleza, 1953), p. 306.

The Gold Rush of the 1690s and the
Early Occupance of Eastern Brazil

The tumultuous rush of people into the wild backlands of interior Minas Gerais in the 1690s is explained in two words: gold fever. The *bandeirantes* from São Paulo had been seeking for over 150 years gold similar to that which the Spaniards had found in Mexico, Peru, Guatemala, and practically all of the territories of Spanish America. The Brazilian El Dorada was finally achieved, at least in the gold-bearing gravels of the Rio das Velhas, northeast of present day Belo Horizonte.

The eastern half of what is now the state of Minas Gerais was composed of fairly infertile metamorphic schists and gneisses, although there were some fertile limestone enclaves to the west (Sete Lagoas) and north (Montes Claros).[3] In the immediate area of the mines were some particularly sterile soils known as the "hunger" schists (*xistos da fome*). As is common in all gold rushes, the early years saw enthusiastic miners who had gold dust in their pockets but nothing to eat. Despite the astronomical prices paid for basic food commodities, many people went hungry. The high prices offered for food at the mining camps had the effect of diverting the food commodities northward from São Paulo and southward from Bahia. All supply currents became deflected toward the gold mining area.

In the early days, the pack trains from the south had to come to the gold fields by way of São Paulo; from Rio de Janeiro, a boat trip was necessary before the trail could be assumed from Paratí or Taubaté, two major junctions along the gold route.

Because so much gold was escaping the royal *quinto* (the "one-fifth" gold tax) and because of the age-old activity of contraband to and from the mines, the Portuguese colonial government decided to build a New Road (literally the *Caminho Novo*) linking the Minas Gerais mines directly with the sea. Rio de Janeiro, the port which served the Minas Gerais hinterland, began to thrive. Rio's location at the end of the gold trail assured its success as a viable urban entity in the eighteenth century.

Some of the people who flocked to the mines were miners from other areas, but there were also some sugar planters (*senhores de engenho*) from Northeast Brazil who made their way southward with their slaves, who they subsequently put to work in the placer gold diggings. Because of the high price of food, some of the sugar planters would have their older and less robust slaves cultivate food crops. Any surplus could be easily sold at a handsome price. In this way some people got out of the gold business and into food production. As the mines petered out, more and more people turned to commercial and subsistence farming; by the nineteenth century, southern Minas Gerais had become a food supplier to the growing metropolis of Rio de Janeiro and other adjacent cities.

[3] Kempton E. Webb, *Geography of Food Supply in Central Minas Gerais* (NAS–NRD), p. 27.

The soil fertility of Minas Gerais is closely tied to the distribution of different types of vegetation, with the *zona da mata* of southeastern Minas Gerais being, historically, the most favored area. Even today, the person from Juiz de Fora or Ubá, is proud to say that he is from the "forest zone." The implication is that the *zona da mata* is the prosperous zone: it is a good address.

The discovery of diamonds in 1630 went almost unnoticed in the midst of all the gold fever, but the yield of diamonds and of gold continues, although at a reduced rate, even today. As the decades passed, the denser populations tended to cluster in those areas of forested lands, with extensive cattle raising taking place mostly in northern Minas Gerais, in the areas with *campo cerrado* (savanna) and *campo limpo* (grasslands).

MINING, INDUSTRIES, AND CITIES IN PRESENT-DAY EASTERN BRAZIL. Although eastern Brazil attained an early reputation from its mineral resources and has continued to benefit from them, it is agriculture that has furnished the livelihood for the great majority of people there. Eastern Brazil consists of the states of Espírito Santo, Minas Gerais, Rio de Janeiro, and the new state of Guanabara (formerly the federal district of Brazil).

We have just seen how the discovery of gold and diamonds provided the needed impulse to draw people into Brazil's interior during the colonial period. The more recent exploitation of iron ore at Itabira, and the manganese mines at Conselheiro Lafaiete have further diversified the mining industry of this part of Brazil.

The agriculture can be closely linked to the vegetation in terms of the capacity of the land to support crops. Leo Waibel has described the gradation of the types of vegetation, east to west, in eastern Brazil.[4] Starting from the east coast, one passes from the first class *mata,* which is the densest, highest form of vegetation, toward slightly drier conditions of second class *mata,* where the trees are more widely spaced, their crowns not so high nor dense. The soils beneath this second class *mata,* which have not been so thoroughly leached, are suitable for farming. Under slightly harsher conditions—less water, more soil acidity—the second class *mata* is followed by the dense savanna vegetation of *cerradão* (a superlative word form meaning a dense *campo cerrado*). The *campo cerrado* is the characteristic savanna or grassland, with scattered trees and bushes, which covers most of the Brazilian west central states of Goias, Mato Grosso, and a large area in northern Minas Gerais. There have been many scholarly debates as to whether the *campo cerrado* is natural or man-made; and its role in the future as a potential breadbasket for Brazil is a fundamental economic question. The *campo cerrado* vegetation has evolved on extremely sterile, acid soils of great antiquity, many of them over a million years old, and has not attracted farmers. In terms of modern farming, however, the *cerrado* areas are easy to manage in that a

---

[4] Leo Waibel, "Vegetation and Land Use in the Planalto Central of Brazil," *Geographical Review* 38(1948): 529–54.

tractor can be driven over them with ease; it appears likely that agricultural activity in this region will increase, but it will require modern management.

The next gradation is the *campo sujo* (literally, "dirty field"), which is a grassland with scattered short trees and bushes. This *campo* is followed by the *campo limpo* ("clean field"), an area of pure grassland. Here, however, the presence of grass does not reflect soil fertility as in the Great Plains of the United States, but rather the extreme sterility of the soil. Only extensive cattle grazing occurs on the *campo limpo*.

The two most dynamic cities in eastern Brazil are Rio de Janeiro and Belo Horizonte. Rio has for many years enjoyed the position of being the primate city of the nation. Only as recently as 1962 has Rio been surpassed by São Paulo in population. Belo Horizonte is interesting because it is the regional capital of a mining area and yet its hinterland, Minas Gerais, is extremely diversified: Minas Gerais is a state of vast mineral wealth and also of increasing agricultural production. Its western *triangulo* area and southeastern *zona da mata* are among the breadbaskets of the country.

Belo Horizonte was a planned capital that was designed and inaugurated in 1897 to provide a central place from which a fast-developing area could expand and flourish. Ouro Preto, the former capital, was too remote to serve as a state capital. In the brief period since Belo Horizonte's inauguration, it has grown from a small village of 14,000 inhabitants to a metropolis of over one million people. As recently as 1956, Belo's population was only half a million. Belo Horizonte is the center of the metallurgical industries and has also attracted other kinds of industry.

Much of eastern Brazil falls within the area called the "Great Region (*Grande Região*) of Rio de Janeiro." Brazilian geographers have undertaken to delimit the hinterland of several Brazilian cities, and the prototype study was done for Rio. The distribution of patients coming to Rio's hospital, of newspapers published in Rio, and of branch offices of banks whose headquarters are in Rio, have been plotted and mapped. The composite map (*opposite*) shows this Grand Region, whose western boundary lies halfway between Rio and São Paulo and whose trend is northward, cutting Minas Gerais in two and leaving the triangle within the economic orbit of São Paulo. The contestant to the north is the city of Salvador, Bahia. Just as Rio has its "Great Region," the interior, smaller cities have their local hinterlands and trading areas. Because of this interdependence between hinterland and the area of central influence in eastern Brazil, the growth of cities has progressed at a very rapid rate (5–6 percent per year) since World War II. Eastern Brazil is one of the most prosperous areas of the country, and it shares with the south the distinction of evolving highly productive and dynamic metropolises.

THE COFFEE FRONTIER OF SÃO PAULO AND ITS INDUSTRIAL HERITAGE. São Paulo is the cultural and economic heartland of Brazil today. The city of São Paulo, like Buenos Aires, experienced most of its incredible growth during the last hundred years. It remained a small provincial town until 1850 when the coffee boom caused it to prosper. Coffee was first grown in the Paraiba Valley, north of Rio de Janeiro. Cultivation spread westward and southward, eventually across the states of São Paulo and Paraná into new areas of virgin forests, or *mata*. A growing world market guaranteed the success of this pioneer area of southern Brazil.

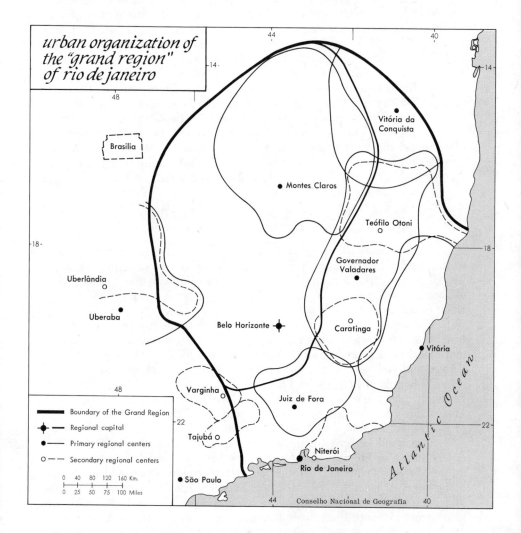

urban organization of the "grand region" of rio de janeiro

Brasilia

Vitória da Conquista

Montes Claros

Teófilo Otoni

Governador Valadares

Uberlândia

Uberaba

Belo Horizonte

Caratinga

Vitória

Varginha

Juiz de Fora

Boundary of the Grand Region
Regional capital
Primary regional centers
Secondary regional centers

0   40   80   120   160 Km.
0   25   50   75   100 Miles

Tajubá

Niterói
Rio de Janeiro

São Paulo

Atlantic Ocean

Conselho Nacional de Geografia

Because of the scarcity of manpower, immigrants were encouraged to come to Brazil, and Italians as well as other Europeans and Japanese took advantage of this opportunity. By 1969 São Paulo state had grown to approximately sixteen million inhabitants, of which over one third, or six million, lived in metropolitan São Paulo.

A number of factors account for the industrial success of São Paulo, for its becoming the leading and most powerful center of industry and manufacturing within all Latin America. First, São Paulo had a source of investment capital, namely the fortunes earned from coffee production since 1850. Second, although peripheral to "settled Brazil" in the colonial period, São Paulo is the center of Brazil's population in the twentieth century. Third, São Paulo has always had an adequate, if not abundant, supply of hydroelectric power due to the far-sighted construction of the hydro-power facilities using the precipitous Serra do Mar escarpment. Fourth, although the city is located on a plateau about 2700 feet high, over-looking the Santos lowland, a cable railway and a modern superhighway have erased any barrier to transportation to its port city of Santos. Some idea of the degree of concentration of industrial activity in São Paulo is revealed by the fact that 30 percent of all Brazilian industry and 40 per-cent of the industrial workers are located in São Paulo state. Most of the markets for São Paulo's industrial production are presently located in eastern and southern Brazil, and especially between the metropolises of São Paulo and Rio de Janeiro. São Paulo city has the highest per capita income and is the richest aggregate market in the entire country.

The South: The Shaping of Southern Brazil by Nineteenth Century European Colonization

The dominant theme in southern Brazil for any geographer, historian, or social scientist is colonization. Southern Brazil is the Portuguese equivalent of Argentina or Uruguay in that it has become essentially European, although to a lesser degree because of the stronger indigenous and essentially Brazilian culture there.

The area is distinguished by its solidly expanding frontier. Agriculture in southern Brazil is the most advanced in the country and follows the more modern practices in other parts of the world. Farmers there use fertilizers and soil conditioners; they plow along the contour and also use selected breeds of animals for higher yields. Southern Brazil is an area of generally high elevations and therefore cool temperatures; it is also an area of fairly fertile soils, such as the weathered diabase lavas in the states of São Paulo, Paraná, and Santa Catarina.

Two main currents of penetration opened up southern Brazil. The *bandeirantes*, or literally "flag-bearers," pushed southward from São Paulo on the *planalto* (plateau). Another current of explorers pushed southward along the coast from São Vicente (near Santos). The first towns of Curitiba and Paranaguá started out as gold mining centers. The early roads in the south were no more than cattle and pack trails over which not only beef cattle but also horses and mules were driven northward, especially during the colonial period, from their breeding grounds in the Rio Grande do Sul and Uruguay.

Rio Grande do Sul was the earliest nineteenth century center of European colonization. The first group of colonists comprised some 20,000 Germans, who came to São Leopoldo in Rio Grande do Sul between 1824 and 1859. They grew rye and potatoes as they had done in Germany because the land in the south was similar in many ways to that of their homeland.

The key to the economic success of São Leopoldo was its accessibility to the markets in Pôrto Alegre, the state capital.

To the north, Santa Catarina became a largely German construction. In 1848 Dr. Herman Blumenau arranged to bring 6000 Germans to the area between 1850 and 1870, and subsequently the Itajaí valley has remained a strong center of German culture. The traveler in this area today hears much German spoken and is able to buy locally printed German language newspapers. The German tradition of frugally-managed, highly-productive small farms operates to supply food for the growing markets in the cities. Towns like Blumenau and Joinville are centers of manufacturing. The state of Paraná also received large numbers of Poles, Russians, and Ukrainians in the years from 1876 to 1879.

The large scale immigration of the Italians occurred between 1870 and 1890. These newcomers established themselves higher up on the *planalto*, located on a diabase *cuesta*, around Caxias do Sul, where they set up small farms and vineyards. On the lowermost areas of the Rio Jacuí valley and its well-watered banks were rice growing areas settled by Portuguese people. The *gaucho* tended his livestock in the extreme southern *campo limpo* grasslands of Rio Grande do Sul. These four main areas are distinct not only in their physical characteristics but also in terms of the culture that has evolved in each area.

In the twentieth century, the spread of coffee has attracted pioneers from other areas of Brazil to the northern and western parts of Paraná, the areas whose diabase soils are free from coffee-killing frosts.

The latest chapter in the story of colonization is the opening up of western Paraná. This is the area to which surplus populations from Rio Grande do Sul have been moving, applying their advanced agricultural techniques to a new area. People from northern Brazil are also relocating there. It will be interesting to observe just how these two different outlooks and attitudes toward land and farming are resolved in the same area of western Paraná.

The Rôdovía do Café (the Coffee Highway), constructed in the mid 1960s in Paraná, represents a bold stroke whereby Paraná is attempting to compete with São Paulo for economic dominance. São Paulo city came to be the regional capital for even northern Paraná because of its easier access, through roads and railroads linking that pioneer zone with the city and its coffee port, Santos. The new highway makes it possible for northern Paraná coffee to pass through Curitiba and on to the coffee port of Paranaguá. This highway has cut travel time from the northwestern parts of Paraná to Curitiba and Paranaguá by 40–50 percent.

Centro Oeste: The Awakened Hinterland of West Central Brazil

This vast interior area of Brazil comprises one-third of the area and only 3 percent of the country's population. Probably more than any other part of the country, this area is considered Brazil's *sertão*. This word *sertão* has a geographical connotation, meaning the dry interior of Northeast Brazil; it also has a generic sense, meaning the mysterious backlands or unknown areas of the country. The basic problem is whether this area will remain a remote hinterland or become a dynamic new center of innovation for Brazil. In many ways, the *centro oeste* of Brazil is in the vanguard of Brazilian developments, largely because of the new capital of Brasília which was inaugurated in April 1960. Formerly on the periphery of the zone of concentrated settlement, west central Brazil now lies directly in the path of Brazil's future and progress.

The early history of west central Brazil is a story of small gold rushes which quickly lost momentum, leaving abandoned mining towns in their wake. The fertile soils eventually found in Minas Gerais, whose cultivation provided an alternative economic development when the gold mines became exhausted, had no equivalent in west central Brazil. This area has remained the domain of the gold and diamond prospectors, as well as that of the extensive cattle raiser who supplies beef to the growing markets of São Paulo and southern Brazil.

Around World War II, a small but important area of fertile forest, the *Mato Grosso de Goiás,* was made accessible by a new road. This oasis of rich potential farmland attracted thousands of new settlers, and southern Goiás has since become a breadbasket not only for Goiás and São Paulo, but for Minas Gerais and Rio de Janeiro as well.

The state of Goiás followed the example of Minas Gerais and moved its capital city from the sleepy colonial mining town of Goiás to Goiânia in 1934; and this, of course, was followed by the move of the national capital from Rio to Brasília in 1960. The main purpose of the new city was to place the national capital in the middle of the country, to stimulate the interior development of Brazil, and to remove the capital from the local interests of the coastal states.

This most unusual phenomenon of establishing a national capital entirely outside the zone of concentrated settlement has already reaped rewards for Brazil. Brasília provides a market destination for the highways radiating inland from the coastal state capitals. Already roads are extending northward from Brasília to Belém and Fortaleza. Some food commodities are coming into Brasília from the areas to the west of the capital over a road that will soon link Brazil with Pucallpa, Peru.

There are still many problems to be resolved with Brasília. Some are political, some geographical, some personal-psychological, for it is difficult to attract people to live in a remote area. Brazilians and most Latin Americans are city lovers if they are not city dwellers: they like the bustle and *movimento* of the city life. Brasília, with its broad avenues and great open spaces, lacks congestion and the sense of *movimento*. Brasília is not a part of traditional Brazilian cities. It is not a city where one gets jostled on the streets by noisy, good-natured crowds. This absence of human contact and togetherness in Brasília is one reason why many people dislike the new capital as a place to live, despite its architectural beauty and careful city planning. Nevertheless, the city remains a symbol of national pride for Brazilians, and it may be that it will ultimately succeed, and for reasons other than those for which it was built.

The agricultural picture of west central Brazil holds little promise if traditional Brazilian farming techniques are maintained. The *campo cerrado* (savanna) requires special techniques in order to be productive. There has been experimental work showing how the acid soils of the *cerrado* can be made productive, with the return on crops equal to three times the cost of rendering the soils productive through fertilizers, soil conditioners, etc. Much of the future of west central Brazil lies in discovering the solution to effective use of the *campo cerrado* for agriculture. Meanwhile, the *campo cerrado* continues to constitute the geographical center of the country.

The Changing Face of the Amazon North

The North of Brazil contains 4 percent of the country's population on almost 42 percent of the land. It is comprised of the two states of Amazonas and Pará, and the four territories of Roraima, Guaporé, Amapá, and Rio Branco.

There are many myths about the Amazon—about its supposedly unbearable climate and boundless resources—but they are mostly inaccurate. The Amazon North is neither as rich nor as poor as legend implies.

Most of the land, the so-called *terra firme*, is fairly flat and is never flooded. Although it is an area of sustained high temperatures, Manaus having a range between 69°F and 98°F, it is the sustained high relative humidities of around 78 percent that make life uncomfortable. Rainfall averages around eighty inches per year over much of the area, but occurs mainly from November to June. Although most of the area is covered by the tropical forest or *selva*, there are considerable areas of *campo cerrado* and grasslands. These open spaces, observable from airplanes, appear to be the result of soil or edaphic factors, rather than climate differences.

Belém was founded as early as 1616, and its easy access to the Amazon River allowed the early Portuguese explorers to probe the interior reaches of the Amazon Basin. Portugal set up a few dyewood gathering stations (*feitorias*) and forts in order to secure the territory from other competing powers, but for the most part, the Amazon North was ignored in favor of Portugal's East Indies ventures. The Amazon North has always been a low priority area within Brazil, although within the last decade efforts have been made through SPVEA (Superintendency for the Economic Valorization of the Amazon) for the valorization and development of the area.

The North had a rubber boom from 1890 to 1913, but it was short-lived and left such reminders of the precariousness of the area's economy as the run-down palatial residences of former rubber barons. You may recall that Charles Goodyear discovered the vulcanization process in 1839. This made rubber much more useful for all kinds of purposes even before automobiles were invented. In 1827 Belém exported some 70,000 pounds of crude rubber; in 1853, it shipped 5,200,000 pounds of rubber. The market suddenly dropped when more efficiently produced rubber from the Malay peninsula successfully competed with Brazilian rubber.

It was believed that if Brazil could also grow rubber on plantations, it would regain a large share of the world's rubber markets. The Ford plantation attempts in Fordlandia and Belterra, near Santarem, failed for a number of reasons ranging from remoteness to plant diseases to unavailability of labor.

In the 1960s the Amazon regained some economic strength and a new basis of economic development with the infusion of government and private investment through tax incentives. The Amazon North became an area of priority within the national goals of regional development. For one thing, the Belém-Brasília highway, opened in 1962, provided the first overland link between that area and the core area of southeastern Brazil. Another road is planned to extend northward from Cuiabá to Santarem. These roads, which have a north-south trajectory, are significant not only because they provide overland communication with the Amazon North but also because the contact comes from a new direction. The general highway plan for Brazil aims to incorporate the Amazon North and other remote areas into the effective national territory. The Amazon River is also part of the highway network through a series of ferries and other transfers.

The modern Amazon includes the manganese mines at the Serra dos Navios in Amapá, where a part of the profits are channelled to IRDA (Regional Institute for the Development of Amapá), which is trying to diversify the economy of that area. A plywood factory has already been established, and research is going on to discover what kinds of commercial plantation crops can be successfully produced in Amapá. The conversion of Manaus to a free port has had a striking impact, although it is too soon to analyze the long-term results of such an action. If oil is ever discovered in quantity in the north, it will radically transform the area.

Cities, Backlands, and the Geography of Brazil's Future

As one looks over the enormous area of Brazil and considers its long history, the sharp discontinuities in both are noticed. There is a basic cleavage today between traditional and modern Brazil, and between urban and rural Brazil.

Traditional Brazil is characterized by low productivity, extensive cattle raising, and subsistence agriculture—the growing of crops such as manioc, which has little nutrient value and which requires large expenditures of energy to produce. Modern Brazil is reflected in the efficiently-grown rice of São Paulo or Rio Grande do Sul and in the modern manganese mines of Amapá. The traditional is reflected in the low-productivity city worker, whether he is a public functionary in an unessential government branch in Rio or whether he is a street vendor in Fortaleza. The new Brazil is distinguished by the increasing number of consumer products available as well as by the application of rational analysis to ordinary problems. The modern approach is to increase productivity: productivity of land, labor, and industry. Traditional Brazil can be summed up as being isolated and feudal, with a small elite group which dominates the social, economic, and political life of the country, submerging masses of poorer people without resources or the means for rising above their positions. The new Brazil is undergoing a profound revolution where improving education and valorizing land through the application of modern technology will result in a wider distribution and greater democratization of economic gain, and, hopefully, greater democratization in a political sense as well.

CHAPTER 11 *middle america: physical and cultural diversity*

Middle America is that part of the Western Hemisphere between the continental United States and South America—Mexico, Central America, and the islands of the Caribbean Sea—that is focused upon the Gulf of Mexico and the Caribbean Sea. Middle America was the first base of New World settlement by the Spaniards. It is a diverse area, with each island and each population nucleus a distinctive composite of physical habitat, people, history, and cultural orientation.

In physical terms, the most dominant feature of Middle America is the Mexican plateau, a great uplifted block of the earth's crust that provides middle-latitude climate in an area mostly within the tropic zone. There is much high ground and mountainous terrain in Middle America, and the well-known phenomenon of vertical zonation (see p. 34) provides a variety of crop habitats. In general, the Pacific side of Mexico and Central America is much drier than the Caribbean or Gulf of Mexico side. This is due to the presence of cold stable air caused by the cold California current. This current, much like the Peru Current along the coast of Peru, chills and stabilizes the air, thus reducing the possibilities for precipitation. On the other hand, the warm water of the Caribbean Sea and the Gulf of Mexico provides abundant moisture to the air which is then carried by the easterly winds, and provides much condensation and rainfall as these winds impinge upon the high slopes of the area.

If one looks at Central America as a whole, one distinguishes not only the basic difference between the dry Pacific and moist Caribbean slopes, but also an asymmetrical slope profile which runs from west to east. A short steep slope faces the Pacific Ocean, and a long gradual slope faces the Caribbean. The amount of rainfall ranges from practically rain-free parts of Baja California to the tropical rainforests of the Miskito Coast in Central America where around 260 inches of rain are recorded yearly. Population densities also vary from zero to over 500 people per square mile in some islands of the West Indies, such as Barbados.

The introductory chapter has already summarized the basic aspects of the Iberian conquest of the New World. In Middle America the conquest occurred with some variations: a higher percentage of the total area of Middle America was settled by Indians compared to the vast reaches of essentially empty land in South America. In the West Indies, nearly all of the Indians were killed off within the first fifty years of Spanish occupance. West and Angelli estimate that in all of Middle America, there may have been as many as fifteen million Indians, all but one million of whom lived on the mainland of Mexico and Central America.[1] The areas of higher culture, as mentioned before, focused upon the central plateau of Mexico, Yucatán, and the highlands and Pacific lowlands of Central America. The Indians of the mainland were reduced in number by diseases, by forced migration, by the diversion of original land away from food production, and by the hard labor exacted in the mines. Wherever possible, the Spaniards tried to pacify and control the Indians by military action, economic pressure, and even by intermarrying with them. Today over half of Guatemala's population and over a tenth of Mexico's still consists of largely unassimilated Indian populations.

The history of Middle America is one in which several nations have sought to leave their mark. At one time or another, Spain, England, France, Netherlands, Denmark, and the United States have competed for power there. There have also been some strong African influences in Haiti and Barbados, and even some Oriental influences such as the East Indians who were brought to Trinidad to replace the slaves as indentured servants. The dominant influence in all these areas, however, was Spanish.

Regarding Middle America as a whole, one is impressed by what a small percentage of the total area is actually cultivated. Most of the people engage in subsistence activities, such as hunting, fishing, gathering, or simple hoe agriculture. The plantations that provide the export crops grow bananas, cacao, and coffee, and involve relatively small numbers of people and areas of land. John Angelli has distinguished the two main areas of Middle America: (*1*) the Euro-African Rimland, essentially the Caribbean area, and (*2*) the Euro-Indian Mainland.[2] The accompanying map shows this distinction.

Mexico

LAND AND LIVELIHOOD BEFORE THE 1910 REVOLUTION.   The Mexico that existed before the 1910 Revolution, during which the breakup of many of the large *haciendas* occurred, had a varied history. After the Wars for Independence from Spain (1810–21), Mexico suffered seventy years of strife before Porfirio Diaz initiated a thirty-three year period of political stability and close economic and technological contact with the United States. This was the period when the Mexican railroads were

---

[1] Robert West and John Angelli, *Middle America* (Prentice-Hall, 1966), p. 5.
[2] West and Angelli, *op. cit.*, p. 11.

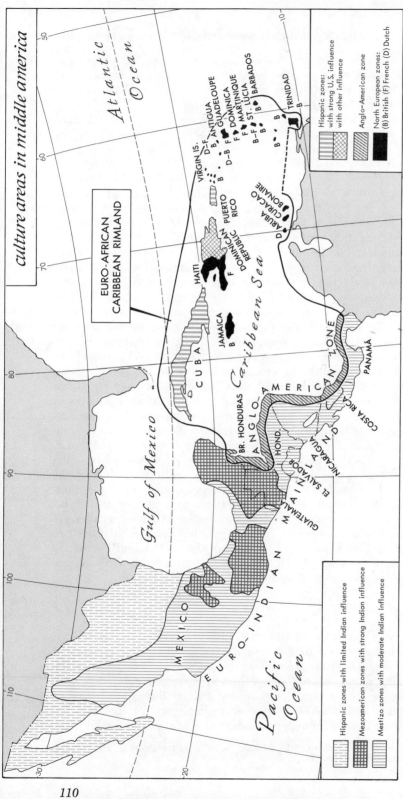

culture areas in middle america

Hispanic zones:
- with strong U.S. influence
- with other influence

Anglo-American zone

North European zones:
(B) British (F) French (D) Dutch

Hispanic zones with limited Indian influence

Mezoamerican zones with strong Indian influence

Mestizo zones with moderate Indian influence

EURO-AFRICAN
CARIBBEAN RIMLAND

Atlantic Ocean

Gulf of Mexico

Pacific Ocean

Caribbean Sea

MEXICO

EURO-INDIAN

GUATEMALA
EL SALVADOR
HOND.
NICARAGUA
COSTA RICA
PANAMÁ

ANGLO-AMERICAN ZONE

BR. HONDURAS

CUBA
JAMAICA B
HAITI
DOMINICAN REPUBLIC
PUERTO RICO
VIRGIN IS.
D-F
B ANTIGUA
B. GUADELOUPE
F DOMINICA
F MARTINIQUE
F ST. LUCIA
B-F BARBADOS
B
TRINIDAD B
D-B
ARUBA
CURAÇAO
BONAIRE
D

*The division of Middle America into Rimland and Mainland sectors
is based primarily on the racial composition of the populations. In
the Caribbean Rimland, where the indigenous people were largely
destroyed during European settlement, European and African strains
dominate. On the mainland, where the original Indian cultures have
had the strongest influence, Indian or part-Indian strains dominate,
with areas of strong Hispanic influence. [From John Augelli, Annals
of the Association of American Geographers, vol. 52 (June 1962),
119–29, by permission.]*

built, mines were revived, and commercial crops such as coffee, sugar cane, and sisal (in Yucatán) were stimulated. Nevertheless, the traditional economic and social patterns persisted with a very small minority controlling most of the productive capacities of the country, and most of the Mexicans having little independence or control over the means of production. Díaz encouraged this pattern: he had the curious habit of giving away parts of the public domain to his personal friends and to some foreigners. Mexico has developed industrially in recent decades but it is still mostly an agrarian economy, with most of the production being of a subsistence nature.

Mexico is favored by having many different raw materials, hydro-electric power, coal, gas, and petroleum deposits, and an abundant labor supply. The Mexican people have sought out the places of greater economic opportunity; this has resulted in fairly large-scale movements of people. Some go to the northern oases, the areas of cotton plantations; some move to the less densely settle farming areas; others move to the cities; and some move to the United States as seasonal farm workers.

POST-REVOLUTIONARY CHANGES ON THE MEXICAN LANDSCAPE. The most important change resulting from the Mexican Revolution of 1910 was the allotment of public lands, called the *ejido*, to private citizens, most of whom were previously landless. The gains from this land distribution, however, have been more of a social and political, rather than economic, boon to the people of Mexico. Subsistence agriculture still continues on a primitive level in many parts of Mexico: the *ejido* has not changed the economic productivity of the people.

The years following the Revolution showed a marked rise in the rate of population growth, as happens in many developing areas where medical benefits have lowered the death rate while birth rates remain high. The average annual population increment had risen from around 1 percent at the time of the Revolution to 3 percent in the late 1960s. Mexico's present population of forty-seven million is expected to reach sixty million by 1975, and eighty-five million by the year 2000. With such a large population growth, the economy must increase output by 3 percent each year just to maintain its present level. To *raise* living standards, however, the economy must increase output more than 3 percent per year.

In the late 1960s Mexico was still two-thirds agrarian and most of its farms were still subsistence operations. Although economic diversification has proceeded with irrigated cotton in the north, coffee and sugar-cane in more well-watered areas, and improved cattle raising techniques, the increases in production are largely offset by the natural population increase.

Since 1945 the pace of industrial development has quickened. There has been an attempt to disperse industry into diverse areas to avoid the classic Latin American pattern of overconcentration of industry in and near the primate city, usually the capital. (An outstanding industrial city is the iron and steel center of Monterrey, just 150 miles from Laredo,

Texas.) An excellent paved highway system facilitates the movement of raw materials in the most densely settled central part of the country. Good roads and railroad connections link central Mexico with the northern deserts and the United States.

Mexico's proximity to the United States and the presence of good road connections have encouraged hundreds of thousands of American tourists to visit Mexico. In recent years, more than half of Mexico's foreign exchange has been earned from tourism.

Central America: An Overview

During the colonial period, the isthmus between Mexico and Panama was known as the Captaincy General of Guatemala. After the Wars for Independence from Spain, in 1821, the Captaincy General became the five states of Guatemala, El Salvador, Honduras, Nicaragua, and Costa Rica. Panama became independent from Colombia in 1903 as the result of the United States plan to build an interocean canal.

Although Spain dominated Central America for 300 years (1500–1800), the United States has dominated its economy ever since. During the nineteenth century, Central America became an actively exploited land of coffee and banana plantations, largely financed and administered by capital investments from the United States.

The total area and population of the six nations of Central America is considerably smaller than most of the larger single countries in Latin America; indeed, there are many states of the larger countries which are far larger in area, and some, such as São Paulo, are comparable in population. Central America is a relatively small area with only about thirteen million inhabitants, most of whom, like their pre-Columbian forbears, live on the Pacific slopes. The average density of population varies from essentially uninhabited areas in some of the eastern forests to around 350 people per square mile in El Salvador to around 1000 per square mile in a few selected areas of Costa Rica. As in Mexico, the annual rates of population growth are very high: 3 percent in Honduras and over 4 percent in Costa Rica, with the other countries having similar increases. Most of the increment is to be found in the growth of cities and also in the few colonization attempts in the eastern forests of the Caribbean slope.

Central America has always been a natural overland route for interocean shipment, and several transisthmus roads have been operating since pre-Columbian times. The most important of these routes are:

1. The Isthmus of Tehuantepec route linking the Pacific Ocean with the Gulf of Mexico;
2. the Guatemala-Puerto Barrios route, today a railroad and highway route, but formerly an important pack trail;
3. the route between Puerto Cortes on the Carribbean coast of Honduras, and the Gulf of Fonseca, a former pirate lair;

4. the route across Costa Rica from Puerto Limón on the Carribbean to Puntarenas on the Pacific;

5. the narrow route across Panama, which finally became the Panama Canal.

The economy of Central America is primarily agrarian. Coffee has been the principal export of Costa Rica, El Salvador, Nicaragua, and Guatemala, and bananas are grown on a few flat and sparsely populated areas of the Caribbean coast in Honduras and the Pacific coast of Costa Rica. Cotton has provided some foreign exchange earnings to Nicaragua, El Salvador, and Guatemala.

The Central American Common Market was organized in 1960 to permit economies of scale and efficient allocations of production facilities among all the Central America countries except Panama. Through lowered tariff barriers and other fiscal and customs arrangements, the Central American republics expect a freer exchange of goods, capital, people, and ideas. There are already some signs that the CACM has been an initial success, although the future of it is very uncertain.

CONTRASTING LAND USES IN GUATEMALA AND EL SALVADOR. Guatemala has the most indigenous population of any Central American country. More than half of the people are Indians, and their strong conservatism has been a complementary equivalent to the conservatism of the traditional landed aristocracy. Great physical diversity characterizes Guatemala, but the great majority of the population lives in the highlands. The Guatemala highlands have always been a zone of intense tectonic activity, with volcanoes and earthquakes having both a constructive and destructive aspect: they provide the fertile weathered lava soils and have also destroyed some cities throughout Guatemala's history. Guatemala, with around four million people, is the most populous Central American city, and its population is growing at the high rate of 3.2 percent per year.

The tropical crops grown by the Guatemalan Indian and mestizo highlanders are maize, beans, and squash, the very same crops grown long before the arrival of the Spaniards. At cooler, higher elevations in the *tierra fría,* some wheat is grown as a cash crop.

El Salvador has the smallest area of the Central American countries and a large population (three million) whose average density is 320 persons per square mile. Its population is increasing by 3.5 percent per year. El Salvador (like Uruguay) is one of the few countries of Latin America where essentially all the land is settled and occupied. There are no geographical frontiers; the effective national territory coincides with the total national territory.

The soils of El Salvador are relatively fertile because of their volcanic origins. Adequate rainfall with a *tierra caliente* climate also assures favorable crop-growing conditions. Commercial agriculture dominates the prime farmland, with coffee, cotton, sisal, and sugarcane being the chief crops; however, most of the 62 percent of the working population are subsistence farmers. El Salvador is a crowded country where the majority of the land and other means of production continue to be owned by a small percentage of the population.

Because of the smaller population of pre-Conquest Indians in this part of Central America, the present population is mostly mestizo. The earliest Spaniards to settle El Salvador were cattle raisers and planters of cacao and the dye-producing indigo.

The pressure of a rapidly expanding population has pushed some farmers into the less densely settled areas east of the Rio Lempa, while people from all parts of the country move to the capital city of San Salvador to seek a livelihood. San Salvador has grown in population from 105,000 in 1940 to 318,000 in 1966. One reason for this growth is the concentration of textile production and other light industry which offer job opportunities. Unfortunately, El Salvador is without energy resources such as coal or petroleum.

HONDURAS AND NICARAGUA. *Honduras* is a large, highly elevated, rugged country with a sparse population. It has about two million people, mostly mestizo, with an average density of forty-five persons per square mile. Honduras is located somewhat outside the main axes of commerce and travel, and its capital, Tegucigalpa, is the only capital city in Central America not located on the Inter-American Highway.

The Honduras highlands are a source of mahogany, oak, and pine. Besides this extractive industry, there is no other kind of land use at the high elevations. The dry Pacific slope had a savanna vegetation as original cover, and there are some problems of water supply during the long dry season characteristic of savanna areas.

Although subsistence farming occupies most of the population, it provides little income. Silver mining was an important source of capital until 1915 when other sources of silver became more important. Commercial agriculture since 1945 has been mainly devoted to coffee on the well-drained volcanic soils of the *tierra templada* and to bananas on the Caribbean coast. Extensive transhumant cattle grazing is carried on, with a kind of migration from highland to lowland pastures depending on the seasons.

Nicaragua has always provided a transisthmian routeway of strategic importance. It has also been favored with productive volcanic soils on the Pacific slope where most of its 1.6 million people live. The large low-lands to the east are sparsely occupied, especially along the wet Misquito Coast where the average annual rainfall is 260 inches per year. About three-fourths of the Nicaraguans are mestizos, with a small proportion of Indians, most of whom live in the humid east. A large majority of the population earns its living directly from the land, although only about 5 percent of the country's total area is actually farmed.

Three broad areas may be distinguished in Nicaragua:

1. The Pacific slope, or core of the country, where most of the people live and where most of the productive activity occurs—the main economic activities being stock raising and the growing of coffee, cotton, and bananas;

2. the central highlands, which are more sparsely settled, and which yield some coffee, cattle, and small amounts of gold and silver;
3. the Caribbean lowlands, which produce bananas and small amounts of gold and wild rubber.

THE ANOMALIES OF COSTA RICA AND PANAMA. *Costa Rica* is cited by Preston James as one of the four areas in Latin America where a solid frontier of settlement has prevailed (the other areas are southern Brazil, the Antioguia part of Colombia, and middle Chile).[3] Today four-fifths of the people of Costa Rica are racially unmixed descendants of Spanish colonists. The republic boasts the highest literacy rate, the most democratic and peaceful government, and highest living standard of all Central America.

Why was this enclave of white Spanish descendants able to persist and build a productive, though small, economy in marked contrast to its neighbors? One reason was that Costa Rica was outside the areas of strong pre-Columbian influence such as Guatemala, El Salvador, western Nicaragua, and Colombia. The few Chibcha-related Indians who were there at the time of the Conquest disappeared, leaving the area wide open for Spanish occupation.

With no available Indian labor, the Spaniards were unable to operate a *latifundio* system. Moreover, since no gold or silver was discovered in Costa Rica, the colonists became farmers. The result was the emergence of a Spanish peasantry engaged in relatively productive subsistence agriculture. Costa Rica's good educational system has meant that a large proportion of the farmers have been able to learn advanced farming techniques. The average farmer in Costa Rica, unlike his counterpart throughout the rest of Latin America, knows how to read and write.

Costa Rica's main regions are:

1. the central highlands where the nation's capital, San José, is located at an elevation of 3500 feet; the densest population lives among the highland valleys;
2. the Pacific lowlands, where the rainfall of 80 to 120 inches per year allows for grazing and the raising of bananas;
3. the Caribbean lowlands, where bananas are raised and the rainfall is somewhat higher (150 to 200 inches per year.)

One-fifth of the country's total population of 1.4 million lives in the environs of San José. Although it is only about 600 square miles, this area is the undisputed culture hearth of the country. The rate of population increase here is one of the highest in Latin America: 4.3 percent per year.

This expansion of population means that the effective national territory has increased from about one-fifth to three-fifths of the country's

[3] Preston E. James, *op. cit.*, p. 6.

total area within the last century. In the first half of the nineteenth century, coffee growing spread throughout the western areas, and banana plantations spread along the Caribbean coast. Between 1930 and 1960 the United Fruit Company shifted its banana operations from the Caribbean to the Pacific coast near Golfito. Cacao plantations have since replaced the former banana production of the Caribbean Coast.

Costa Rica is essentially an agricultural country whose exportable cash crops are coffee, bananas, and cacao. The average coffee *finca* (plantation), smaller than those in other Latin America countries, has an area of less than twenty-five acres. It is sufficient to support one family at a reasonably satisfactory living standard.

Industrial production is small, and mostly concentrated around San José. Typical light industries produce processed foods, textiles, shoes, and clothing. A nitrogen-producing plant was built in Puntarenas in 1963 and will furnish fertilizer for the country; a French-built petroleum oil refinery was completed in 1965 and will economize on the country's foreign exchange expenditures.

Panama formed a part of Colombia until 1903, when it became an independent country, and thereby facilitated the United States' objective of building an interocean canal, since the United States could deal with Panama more easily than it had been able to with Colombia. Panama still has no land connection to Colombia—only sea and air transport link the two countries.

The lifeblood of Panama is the Panama Canal. One-third of the 1.2 million people in the country live within the ten-mile-wide Panama Canal Zone, which is leased to the United States for 99 years and is controlled by the United States Government. The capital, Panama City, adjoins the Canal Zone, and Balboa lies just inside the Zone on the Pacific end of the Canal. Colon and its port city of San Cristobal lie at the Caribbean end of the fifty-mile-long canal. The Canal, with the business and commerce it generates, is the dominant element in the Panamanian economy. This overdependence has been a source of discontent for many Panamanians who wish to become more independent from the overwhelming influence of the United States.

The two main areas of Panama are: (*1*) the transit zone, which is urban and cosmopolitan and is racially mixed; and (*2*) the Pacific lowland, which, existing apart from the Canal, is a typically rural and agrarian area of Central America. Most of Panama's population is racially mixed, mulatto or mestizo, with about 15 percent Negro, 6 percent Indian, and 12 percent whites.

The Canal Zone is an eloquent example of the kind of comfortable and healthy living conditions that can be created within the humid tropics *if* the investment is justified, as it is in the case of Panama by the Canal. The problem with most areas of the humid tropics is that they do not promise an economic return great enough to justify the added cost, especially in the hierarchy of economic, social, and strategic priorities of countries with limited physical, human, and capital resources.

CHAPTER 12   *the caribbean area*

The Physical Base of the Caribbean Antilles

The geological structure of the islands, large and small, of the Caribbean Sea is closely related to the mainland geological lineaments of Mexico, Central America, and northern South America. Many of the east-west–trending ridges and depressions of Chiapas in Southern Mexico, and the highlands of Guatemala and Honduras disappear under the Caribbean waters only to reappear in the east-west–trending mountains of the Sierra Maestra of Cuba, the Blue Mountains of Jamaica, and the corresponding alignments of highlands and depressions of Hispaniola. The northernmost, east-west oriented mountains of Trinidad are but an outlier of the Venezuelan Andes. The limestone platform which forms the base of the easternmost portions of the Lesser Antilles is geologically related to the shallow limestone platform of recent geological age which comprises the Yucatán Peninsula and the state of Florida.

Altitude above sea level and orientation and exposure to moisture-carrying eastern winds are the two dominant controls upon the Caribbean climate. The warm water temperatures (73°F to 84°F) of the Gulf of Mexico and the Caribbean Sea provide abundant moisture to the prevailing winds, and this moisture is condensed whenever the winds are forced to rise over a sufficiently high land surface. The low mountains of Puerto Rico are high enough to cause high orographic precipitation whereas the low-lying (less than 600 feet elevation) limestone platform of Yucatán is not high enough to cause rainfall. In general, the eastward-facing, windward mountain slopes of the Caribbean islands receive heavy rainfall while the leeward slopes lie in the rain shadow and exhibit drier and even pronounced xerophytic effects on vegetation.

The original vegetation pattern closely follows the rainfall distribu-

117

tion, with all windward slopes covered by lush verdant forests. The forest-clearing activities of man over the past 400 years have removed most of the original vegetation and left a sparser, more xerophytic cover. Only in the more inaccessible, steeper areas of little economic value do reminders of the original verdure remain. Elsewhere, man has planted subsistence crops and commercial crops such as sugarcane, and coffee, while the lower priority lands have been turned over to extensive cattle grazing.

The richest soils for farming are in the few areas of azonal alluvial soils along the river floodplains, as in the northern Dominican Republic, some areas of weathered lavas, as in the lesser Antilles, and a few lime-stone areas, such as interior Jamaica. Elsewhere, soils of modest fertility have been so abused and eroded by wasteful cultivation and overgrazing on sloping land that the productive soil base is in jeopardy.

The Cultural Geography of the Antilles

The cultural geography of the Caribbean area is a complex mosaic of different cultural groups settling different areas at various times. We can distinguish four main cultural divisions, each corresponding with a particular time period.

The first was the pre-Columbian period during which a succession of distinct cultural waves from the mainland influenced the people and their ways of life on the islands. Out of these early years came the peaceful Arawak Indians, who were concentrated on the larger islands, and the more warlike Carib Indians of the smaller islands and fringe areas. It was these people whom the Spanish *conquistatores* first encountered and soon eliminated around 1500 A.D.

The second major period was that of military conquest and Europe-anization through Spanish settlement, between 1500 and 1700. You have already become familiar with many aspects of the Spanish colonial administration in the introductory chapters of this book.

The third period, and the most influential in terms of contemporary history, was that based upon the sugar plantation system and slave labor which dominated the social and economic life of the area between 1700 and 1890.

The fourth period is that of the modern plantation, a system which has prevailed into the twentieth century. These four periods provide the dominant influences around which national and everyday life revolved. Of course, the middle years of this century mark greater economic diversification of the Caribbean area through increasing industrialization and tourism so that the traditional yardsticks for evaluation of the area (such as export of cash crops) are themselves changing.

The island of Hispaniola was the first base for Spanish settlement and exploration, as well as exploitation, in Middle America. The Spaniards sought and mined ephemeral gold deposits during the brief period from 1496 to 1520, and moved their base from Isabela on the north coast of present-day Dominican Republic to the present-day site of Santo Domingo on the south coast.

The first English conquest of any consequence in the Caribbean was that of Jamaica in 1655 when there were only about 1500 Spaniards there to guard the island. The little gold there had long since been exhausted and the few Indians eliminated by the 1630s. The lack of a labor force prevented any meaningful exploitation of Jamaica until African slaves were brought in during the sixteenth century. Nevertheless, sugar growing became profitable only in the nineteenth century when large plantations with their economies of scale were established. With the eventual decline of sugarcane, the economy of Jamaica is now based largely on subsistence farming, some extensive grazing, and a few locally important industrial, mining, and tourist centers.

Whereas the English managed to claim St. Kitts, the British Virgin Islands, the Bahamas, and Trinidad during the seventeenth and eighteenth centuries, the French acquired Martinique, Guadeloupe, and Haiti. The Dutch acquired Aruba, Curaçao, and Bonaire. Spain, however, continued to dominate the general Caribbean area by retaining Cuba, Puerto Rico (until ceded to the United States in 1898 as a result of the Spanish-American War), and the surrounding mainland areas and other small islands.

The post-World War II period, and especially the 1960s, has witnessed a strong development within the entire Caribbean area in the tourist industry. In common with Mexico, the West Indies have especially fostered the building of resort hotels in order to lure vacationers from the snowy northern winters of the United States, Canada, and Europe. The tourist industry has become the key economic mainstay of the West Indies.

Each of these small fragments of Latin America has unique problems, and each faces special problems in surviving as a small political unit within a zone of politically fragmented pieces. The problems of small areas, including the three Guiana territories of Guyana, Surinam, and French Guiana, are inherently different from the problems of the large mainland countries. The abortive attempt to establish a West Indies Federation underlines the imposing obstacles to political and economic integration of physically, geographically, economically, and culturally discrete political areas.

conclusions

Latin America is unique among the major developing areas of the world in that dynamic cultural changes are perceptible within a single generation; revolutionary modifications of people's lives and livelihoods can be traced in a lifetime.

What will happen to Latin America in the decades to come? Can the fundamental problems of earning a livelihood, producing sufficient food, and developing effective government for all the people be solved to any degree? With such rapidly growing populations (and there is little hope to expect a drastic reduction in the fertility rate), can most Latin American economies ever run fast enough to keep from retrogressing economically?

The outlook is not hopeful. Although the complex problems of ecological destruction, urban slum growth, inflation, population expansion, and the governing of thinly-populated areas may be understood in large part, it is not at all obvious that Latin American countries can organize economic resources and apply the technological, political, and social solutions to ward off major crises within the next twenty years. If developed countries such as the United States cannot handle these problems, even today, how can developing countries be expected to succeed on a much smaller economic base?

By the end of the century, it may happen that the national qualities of character and independence will weigh more heavily than national economies in determining which national states and styles will prevail in the next century. Latin America is evolving in fascinating and varied ways. The history of the interaction between man and land, between society and the physical environment in Latin American should help us view the contemporary processes of landscape and societal change with some understanding. As we accompany Latin America through the remaining years of this century, in a world where distances are diminishing and our interdependence is increasing, we should be aware that the fate of Latin America marks our own.

appendix

Table 1. Principal Pre-Columbian Domesticated Plants and Animals in the Highland Area

Common Name	Botanical Name	Occurrence
SEED CROPS		
Maize	*Zea mays*	All Areas
Lupine	*Lupinus tauris*	Highlands
Quinoa	*Chenopodium quinoa*	"
Canahua	*Chenopodium pallidicaule*	"
Amaranth	*Amaranthus*	"
BEANS		
Kidney	*Phaseolus vulgaris*	General
Scarlet runner	*Phaseolus multiflorus*	Cauca River
Lima	*Phaseolus lunatus*	Coast
Jack	*Canavalis ensiformis*	Coast
FRUITS		
Pineapple	*Ananas sativus*	Tropical
Soursop	*Annona muricata*	Lowlands
Pepino	*Solanum muricatum*	Temperate
ROOTS		
Potato	*Solanum tuberosum*	Chile Coast
Potato	*Solanum andigenum*	Highlands
Oca	*Oxalis tuberosa*	"
Ulluco	*Ullucus tuberosus*	"
Mashua	*Tropaeolum tuberosum*	"
Achira	*Canna edulis*	Coast; temperate valley
Arracacha	*Arracacia xanthorrhiza*	Temperate valleys
Yacon	*Polymnia edulis*	"
Yuca (sweet manioc)	*Manihot*	Tropical lowlands
Peanut	*Arachis hypogaea*	Lowlands
Sweet Potato	*Ipomoea batatas*	Tropical lowlands
MISCELLANEOUS		
Squash	*Cucurbita maxima*	General
Peppers, aji	*Capsicum annuum*	Medium climates
Cacao	*Theobroma cacao*	Low valleys
Cotton	*Gossypium hirsutum*	Tropical Coast
Cotton	*Gossypium barbadense*	Coast
NARCOTICS		
Tobacco	*Nicotiana tabacum*	General
Tobacco	*Nicotiana rustica*	Highlands
Coca	*Erythroxylon coca*	Warm valleys

ANIMALS
Llama, alpaca, dog, guinea pig, and Muscovy duck

Table 2. Principal European-Introduced Plants and Animals

PLANTS

Wheat
Barley
Alfalfa
Sugar Cane
Grapes
Fruits (citrus fruits, apples, peaches, apricots, almonds, plums, date palms, figs,
    pomegranates, quinces, olives, bananas)
Vegetables of the garden variety (cabbage, lettuce, squashes, and turnip)
Nuts from New Spain
Garlic

ANIMALS

Cattle	Horses
Pigs	Mules
Sheep	Pigeons
Goats	Camels
Chickens	Guinea hens
